INNER BEAUTY IS
WHAT COUNTS

INNER BEAUTY IS WHAT COUNTS

I Athrobia En I Omorkia

(Greek Cypriot translation)

Η αδρωπια εν η ομορκια

DEMETRAKIS (JIM) IOANNOU

Copyright © 2015 by Demetrakis (Jim) Ioannou.

Library of Congress Control Number: 2015913462
ISBN: Hardcover   978-1-5035-0913-9
               Softcover   978-1-5035-0912-2
               eBook   978-1-5035-0911-5

All rights reserved. No part of this book may be reproduced or transmitted in any form or by any means, electronic or mechanical, including photocopying, recording, or by any information storage and retrieval system, without permission in writing from the copyright owner.

This is a work of fiction. Names, characters, places and incidents either are the product of the author's imagination or are used fictitiously, and any resemblance to any actual persons, living or dead, events, or locales is entirely coincidental.

Any people depicted in stock imagery provided by Thinkstock are models, and such images are being used for illustrative purposes only. Certain stock imagery © Thinkstock.

Print information available on the last page.

Rev. date: 09/21/2015

To order additional copies of this book, contact:
Xlibris
1-800-455-039
www.Xlibris.com.au
Orders@Xlibris.com.au
710848

Reflecting, reminiscing and reciting proverbs on life's lessons: a happy and useful experience to be had!

Men and women who have had many experiences in life are usually our grandfathers and grandmothers. Hence, their children and grandchildren (should) go to them for advice when faced with a problem of the mind or a puzzle of the heart. Why do we go them? Because we know that they have turned their life experiences into a mature wisdom and they are ready and willing to share that wisdom. It is a fact of life that wisdom can be gained by constantly reflecting on many years of living and seeking to live through rich experiences. It is also a fact of life that our ancestors leave behind them so much wisdom that we sometimes collect, record and value. Sometimes we reflect on the wisdom of the old once we have lost them, but then, ironically, we realise that what we lost was more valuable than we originally thought; we could have learned a lot from them, but it is too late.

Fortunately, Jim Ioannou falls in the first category of the people I mention. Namely, he realised early that he can learn a lot from his ancestors, his father and mother but above all, form his "wise, open-minded, kind, generous and honest grandfather," priest Efthimios, his "grandfather and mentor" from the Cypriot village of Ora. What a lucky man is Jim Ioannou to have a grandfather like priest Efthimios; with so many qualities and virtues! Who wouldn't want to have a grandfather like father Efthimios!

After reading *"Inner Beauty is What Counts" by* Jim Ioannou, I came to the conclusion that father Efthimios has certainly passed one of his virtues to his grandchild, Jim Ioannou. The virtue is that of generosity. It is indeed a generous and selfless act by a person to spend months and years to collect from many people and many experiences, so many folk proverbs, record them, record life experiences related to those proverbs and present them to the reading public in the form of a gift of wisdom.

This book is full of many wise folk proverbs, made by the people for the people. The people who created these proverbs certainly saw that life is full of meaning, full of lessons and full of wisdom that must not be forgotten. Thus, they turned their wisdom into proverbs. In these folk proverbs, I observe language techniques that make me admire them. Their common characteristics are: brevity, metaphor, impact. The author provides examples of how these proverbs have been used in moments of time and in peoples' lives, and this gives the book another quality, that of usefulness. It was the famous ancient Greek playwright Aeschylus (525-456 B.C.) who said: "Wise is the person who knows useful things, not many things." The reader of this book will therefore gain useful knowledge of a wisdom that was derived over many years during which the common people, turned the lessons they learnt from everyday life into a short and sweet summary, called a proverb. This book is therefore entertaining, pleasant and useful for any reader, young and old.

The author reminisces on some humorous and some ironic (but never demeaning) reflections of simple life among simple people, when they make mistakes, they misjudge or misconstrue people, actions or ideas. The reader will find these moments engaging because the proverb that applies to each moment will invite the reader to reflect on their personal moments when they made mistakes and they could have done things differently. The experience of reading this book becomes therefore a didactic one. It was the ancient Greek philosopher Plato (427-347 B.C.)

who taught us that "wisdom is a virtue; ignorance is the root of all evils." The younger generation will find that by reading *"Inner Beauty is What Counts"* they will realise how much wisdom the older generations created and how much they still need to catch up with that wisdom, which is summarised in the proverbs and the stories of this book.

Finally a word about the language used in this book. Let us remember what the great author and poet William Butler Yeats (1865-1939, Nobel Laureate 1923) left us in his legacy: "Think like a wise man but communicate in the language of the people." The language of the book is simple as it speaks about simple characters who learn from everyday experiences. The wisdom though that is the final conclusion of each experience makes the language enjoyable and engaging; it made me want to read further, to learn more and to be entertained at the same time. Wisdom and knowledge is after all a happy experience. I was enriched and I was happy to have read this book and I believe the reader will feel the same way! The content of the book is really a reflection on the inner beauty of human beings who learn while they live.

John Milides
Academic
Deakin University

15th July, 2015

Dear Jim

Re: INNER BEAUTY IS WHAT COUNTS

I commend you for working hard to collect all those "παροιμίες" (Proverbs) which enrich our tradition and culture. They are also very didactic not only for the young who will benefit because they have never been acquainted but for the elderly too who have forgotten them.

Thanks,

Constantinos Procopiou.

President of the PANAUSTRALIAN JUSTICE FOR CYPRUS COORDINATING COMMITTEE (PA.S.E.K.A.) and Acting president of the Australian/Hellenic Council, (AHC).

SUMMARY OF THE BOOK
INNER BEAUTY IS WHAT COUNTS –
(Η ΑΝΘΡΩΠΙΑ ΕΙΝΑΙ Η ΟΜΟΡΦΙΑ)

When we hear *Parimies* (Greek for proverbs and sayings) we often say *"I remember my grandmother saying that"*, but we probably never fully captured the power and depth of these words. Even though the young generations of migrants of the diaspora may have been exposed to the language of the *Parimies* by their parents and grandparents, the beauty and strength of the messages, was only vaguely understood as the next generations experienced a language barrier which prevented full comprehension and appreciation of these proverbs.

During my childhood, *Parimies* comprised a rich part of my parents' and grandparents' vocabulary who often conveyed messages to us through the powerful tool of these proverbs. The wisdom, philosophy and logic of the *Parimies* fascinated me as a young boy. I made a promise to myself that one day I would present these ancient gems in a way which I hope will ignite a spark of inspiration to be carried through to future generations.

Well, this is what this book is all about. I have stayed true to my goal and after four years of research and hard work, I put before you every aspect of the fascinating world of the *Parimies*. I hope that the humour and sadness of the stories used as examples (mainly true stories from my own life experience) will resonate with you dear reader and give you an insight of the richness of the Greek /Cypriot culture family values and life in general. It's the kind of book that you will come back to from time to time and I truly hope that it will find a very special place in your personal library.

The Author

Jim Ioannou

Acknowledgement

Four years was a long journey to bring this book to completion and I would like to thank all my friends and family for their contribution, particularly the retired teacher, my friend, **Harry Shiamaris** for the long hours he worked to do the Greek spelling check and **Katie Georgiou** for the supply of valuable information.

A huge thanks to the professors from **Deakin University** Melbourne **Mr John Milides and also Mr Costas Procopiou** for making the time to read the book and for their kind words of endorsement and encouragement.

I remember when I was a young elementary school pupil in my home village, there was a little picturesque village called Ora, on the island of Cyprus – forty minutes' drive from Larnaca Airport; it is an absolute joy to see the magical view of Ora, as you approach through the winding road.

Ora, Cyprus

Its stone houses with the red ceramic roofs, scattered across the slopes of the mountains, as well as the greenery of surrounding olive trees, give a sense of tranquillity and peace. In those days (late 1950s) there were no electricity, television, computers, and mobile telephones.

We had dinner together as a family every day, and then we would gather around the fireplace, under the dimmed light of a kerosene lamp, and listen to our parents or grandparents telling us stories and *parimies*, the Greek word for proverbs. It was an occasion to spend quality time together and interact with one another.

My grandfather, Papa Efthimios, my mother's father, who was the then priest of the village, was my mentor during the developing years of my life.

He was a wise and open-minded man, with above-average intelligence, wisdom, and general knowledge. He was known for his kindness, generosity, and honesty and was very well respected in the region.

When he was young, in the early 1900s, he migrated to United States of America, looking for a better life. When he returned to the village he decided to become a priest and was ordained in 1923. Even though he was a cleric, he never allowed fundamentalism to influence logic. He was open-minded, and he always used logic and consideration when he made decisions. I looked up to him and admired him for that.

My grandfather and mentor, Papa Efthimios, with my grandmother, Elpitha

Papa Efthimios as well as my mother often used parimies to convey a message and to make a point. They were effective and educational and often became the point of interesting discussions. The positive effect they had on me, particularly during my teenage years, was phenomenal.

In 1962, at the age of twelve, I left the village to begin my high schooling in Larnaca at Dianellios Technical School and then went to Johannesburg, South Africa, after completing a compulsory two-year army training in Cyprus in 1969.

In my School uniform of Dianellios Epanggelmatiki Sholi Larnacos
1967 Graduate
Known as Dimitriou Dimitrios Ioannou

In 1972, I met my wife Irene, who was born in Australia of Greek–Cypriot parents. They were born in Lysos, Cyprus, and were on holiday visiting her five uncles and aunties in Johannesburg and Benoni at the time (the Charalambous, Xinisteris, and Jasonidis families).

A year later we got married at the Greek Cathedral church of St Constantino's and Eleni in Johannesburg. We had two children, Christalene and Angelo, and a couple of years later, in 1977, we moved to Melbourne, Australia, to reunite with her parents and the rest of her extended family.

Ω

The Power of Proverbs

In the last few centuries, Cyprus and Greece in general have been occupied by various conquerors. During that time schooling was almost impossible and the standard of education was poor; therefore, it was the responsibility of parents and grandparents to teach their offspring general knowledge and to equip them with survival skills which would better their standard of living. The only way they knew how was through *proverbs.*

I don't want to sound like a historian, but some of them go back to Egyptian civilisation 1500 BC. Proverbs were created from our ancestors' life experiences and wisdom and passed on from generation to generation. Personally, I consider them to be the 'commandments of life', and according to the legacy, each one of them had been composed and delivered after forty days of fasting. I believe this is a metaphorical expression emphasising the great deal of effort, consideration, and wisdom put into them.

The most important characteristic of proverbs, apart from wisdom and philosophy is their power to help make a point, even in short conversations on the road. They are short and easy to remember because of the poetic way in which they are written – that is in verse and rhyme – and are often satirical and mocking.

An example of how easy it is for someone to make a point with a proverb is this popular English proverb 'If you pay peanuts, you get monkeys'. This means, of course, that if you pay less to get a job done you may not get it done in the way you expected. Many people also use it when you buy something cheap, usually of poor quality that will not last long.

Another example is 'Don't put all your eggs in one basket'. In other words, divide them into a few baskets so that if you drop one, you won't smash all of them. This advice is often given by financial advisors to their clients who wish to invest money is to divide it in to more than one portfolio.

Moral
If you want to reduce risk, don't put everything in one place or rely on one person, or one plan of action.

One of the greatest benefits of proverbs is the flexibility to be used in more than one context or set of circumstances. While they occasionally may appear to contradict each other, these are generally exceptions, like with any rule.

With today's technology, computers, Internet, and all the information that's available at our fingertips, some might thing that parimies are a thing of the past, but there is one important thing that we should never forget. Technology is based on mathematics, geometry, physics, and other scientific principles which we inherited from scientists of past generations such as Archimedes, Newton, Einstein, and Hippocrates. It doesn't matter what language we speak, in which era we live, or how we obtain the information; times change, methods change, technology changes, but the principles and rules of nature don't change. Two plus two equals four, no matter how advanced technology is.

Pythagora's theory will never change regardless of whether it is calculated manually or electronically or any other way. Most proverbs are based on the same principles of nature, and they will always be valid.

If you spend more than what you earn, you will always be short of money, regardless of how much money you make.

About the Title

The title of this book, *I athropia en i omorkia,* is my new proverb.

In Greek–Cypriot dialect this means 'The inner beauty is what counts in a person'. It is something that I wholeheartedly believe in and the reason I used it as a title. It is also similar to the English proverb 'Don't judge the book by its cover', or the Greek Filotimo. In my opinion, *I athropia en i omorkia* is a very important proverb. It's inner beauty that makes a person beautiful and not the outer physical appearance.

Simply put, you can be the prettiest person on earth, that is, until you open your mouth and make a comment, or vice versa. Of course, if the outer appearance is as beautiful as the inner that's a bonus, for as long as it lasts.

'Inner beauty can be described as something pleasant, experienced through one's character rather than by appearance' (Wikipedia).

If we pay too much attention to the outer appearance, we could end up being very disappointed and unhappy as time passes, either with ourselves, our partner, or friends because people change as they grow older. Nature has to take its course, and nothing can stop the ageing process. We can go bald or become grey, overweight, and wrinkly or even be affected with some kind of disability. If we can see and value the inner beauty of a person, it would be a charisma that could bring us happiness and satisfaction, not to mention the happiness we would give to others, simply because *outer beauty doesn't last for life. Inner beauty does.*

Sappho, the most famous female lyric poet of the ancient Greek world (500 BC), once said, 'Beauty endures only for as long as it can be seen, goodness beautiful today, will remain so tomorrow.'

Nothing has changed since then, and nothing can be changed about it, regardless of what your religion is, or what your spiritual and social morals or ethics are. Each religion has good and bad people. It doesn't necessarily mean that when you are religious and a regular churchgoer you are automatically a good person or if you are not you are automatically a bad person. I know many good people that are not religious at all, or their religion or race is different from ours, yet they are kind, helpful, giving, and not judgemental. What is important is to have the ability to respect other people's beliefs, value their inner beauty, and treat everyone the way we wish to be treated.

Cover Picture – The Eye

The cover picture is of my son Angelo's eye. The eye symbolises the window through which one can 'see' in and out of the human body.

The Lying Eyes (True story)

I remember once I went out in my back yard to inspect my vegie patch and noticed some of my tomato plants broken. My son Angelo was five years old; then I called him outside and asked him if he knew anything about it. He said, 'No, Daddy, I don't know.' I then asked him to come closer and look at me in the eyes. I said, 'Who kicked the basketball in the vegie patch and snapped the tomatos?' He then replied, 'I did, Daddy. I am sorry.' I then sent him in his room, and his punishment for lying was to go to bed one hour earlier than his usual bedtime. The next day after school my daughter Christalene came up to me and asked if I can tell her the secret. I said what secret? She said, 'How you can tell that Angelo is lying by looking at his eyes?' I laughed and said, 'When a person lies, his pupils grow larger.' She shook her head happily that she knew the secret and walked away. A week later my wife told me that Angelo pushed his cousin Ody off the bike. I called him up and asked him if that was true, and without lifting his head up, he said no. He was avoiding direct eye contact so I wouldn't see his pupils. It was hilarious, and I couldn't stop laughing. I gave him a hug and told him the parimia of the little shepherd crying wolf. (O voscos o pseftis). I think that really had an effect in him.

Proverbs and Sayings

Each Proverb in This Book Is Structured as Follows:

1. **Proverb** *in Greek using English characters*

2. **Proverb** in Greek. Using Greek characters

3. **Proverb** and everything else hereafter are in English

4. **Meaning** of proverb

5. **Used –** Where and when the proverb can be used

6. **Examples** of how a proverb is used (with author's comments and many true stories)

7. **Moral** of proverb

For accurate pronunciation refer to the phonetics chart at the end of this book.

A

1. *Agooe yeroo simvoolin, je bethevmenoo ynosin.*
1. Άκουε γέρου συμβουλήν τζαι παιδευμένου γνώσην.
1. Take old man's advice and academic's knowledge.

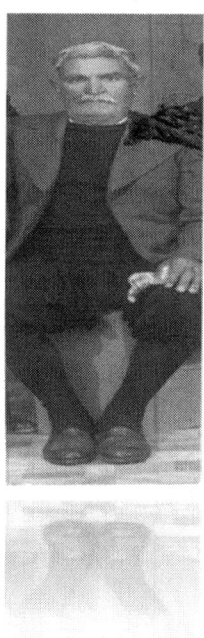

My grandfather (bappoo) Dimitros Kyriakou

Meaning
Taking the advice of an experienced or an academic person can increase your chances of succeeding.

Used
Used when one works on an unfamiliar project, doesn't seek advice from a knowledgeable person and makes mistakes that could have been avoided.

Example
Joseph was a young man that started a new business importing tables and chairs from China. The chairs where polished but unassembled and were assembled in a workshop. One day I went to visit him in the warehouse, and when I saw the way they were assembling the chairs, I said to Joseph that the way in which he was putting them together would mean the chairs would fall apart. He didn't take any notice and gave me a dirty look, taking offence to what I had said. He responded, 'We have been doing it this way for six months, and we have not had any complaints.' I apologised and told him he obviously knew what he was doing.

Eighteen months later I went passed the warehouse again, and it was closed. A few months later we met at the furniture show and I asked if they had moved. He said, 'No, I had to close the business down.' I wasn't surprised by that but asked him to tell me about it. He confessed that they had too many problems with the chairs falling apart and people falling off and getting hurt. He said he had many lawsuits from customers claiming compensation for their back and other injuries, which forced him into bankruptcy and he lost everything.

After a short pause he looked at me and said, 'Now I know what the problem was, and I wish that you kicked me between my legs to listen to you then.'

That's when Bappoo says, *'Agooe yeroo simvoolin, je bethevmenoo ynosin.'*

Moral
Informed decisions are more accurate.

It is wise to consult an experienced and knowledgeable person before you do something that you are not familiar with.

The Intersection of Evil and Virtue

Talking about advice, I remember soon after my twelfth birthday as the date of my departure to begin my schooling was getting closer, my mother was already getting worried about me. One day she sat next to me with tears in her eyes told me that I was going to be out there alone, in a world of many challenges, risks, and temptations. She then took my hand in her hand and with her index finger drew a T in my palm.

She then looked at me and said, 'You have now come to this T intersection. If you take the left turn it will take you to *kakia* (evil), and if you take the right, it will take you to *areti* (virtue). You must now choose which path you will follow.'

Without any hesitation, I replied, 'I choose to turn right towards Areti, because I want to be a good, honest, and a law-obeying citizen.' She then put her arms around me, kissed me, and gave me her blessings (*din efjin moo n'ashis yiokka moo*). This picture still is and will remain in my mind for life.

As far as I am concerned it was the frame of mind that she put me in that always guided me to the right road.

My mum shelling fresh almonds, 1983

It has taken me a long time to realise how powerful the message of this story is and the positive effect that it had on me. Every time I was in a dilemma I knew I had to turn right.

*2. Aboo libade doo gattoo do lardin,
dron da rooha doo i bondiji.*
2. Απού λυπάται του κάττου το λαρτίν
τρών τα ρούχα του οι ποντιτζοί.
2. If you don't feed the cat, your
clothes will be eaten by mice.

Meaning
If you do not invest in cat food, you will lose the cat and then the mice will eat your clothes.

Used
Used when one is stingy to spend money on essentials, and as a result of that, one incurs more losses.

Example
Christos the grape farmer underpaid his grape pickers. He wasn't even paying them for overtime despite all their complaints. They were so unhappy that they all resigned before the job was compleeted. By the time he organised other pickers, his crop was destroyed by bad weather, and he lost it all. That's when

Bappoo says, '*Aboo lib**a**de doo g**a**ttoo do lard**in**, dron da r**oo**ha doo i bondij**i**.'

Moral
Give more to receive more.

3. *Anifandaris ditsiros, tsangaris alibolidos.*
3. Ανυφαντάρης (υφαντης, ράφτης) τίτσιρος, τσαγκάρης αλυπόλητος.
3. Naked tailor, barefoot shoemaker.

Meaning
A tailor who doesn't have clothes and a shoemaker who doesn't have shoes.

Used
Used mainly when trades people neclect themselves because they put customers first.

Example
A motor mechanic has problems with his own car because he is too busy to fix it. You can then say, *'Anifandaris ditsiros, tsangaris alibolidos.'*

Moral
Pay yourselves first.

My Children Taught Me a Lesson

This reminds me of a story that happened when my children were very young, and I can't resist sharing it with you.

I was a workaholic for many years, going to work very early in the morning before my kids were awake and returning late at night when they were asleep. I would only see them once a week, on a Sunday. I would always justify my work to my wife, saying that I was doing it for her and the children, to give them a better future. I was worried about the mortgage on the house, about our finances, and other primary material things. My wife kept on saying, 'What's the point of working, if you can't spend time with your family?'

My family and I outside our first Melbourne home in 1979
My wife Irene, Christalene 6, and Angelo 5.

I couldn't see that as I was too involved with the running of the business, until one day something happened that shook my inner world. It was like being hit by a lightning bolt which woke me up from a coma.

It was early afternoon of the 26 June 1981. My new furniture designs were ready, and we were preparing the showroom for a new product selection meeting, with a large national retail chain. They were to select new lines for their next quarterly catalogue, and you can understand how important that was for our company. I was in charge of the presentation, and the pressure was on my shoulders. Suddenly I was called into the office to take a call from my daughter, Christalene.

'Hello, sweetheart,' I said.

'Hello, Daddy,' she replied in an unusually low voice suggesting sadness.

I said, 'What's the problem, darling?'

After a short pause, she said, 'Daddy, it's my birthday today. I am seven years old. Can you come home early tonight, please?'

I froze. My hair stood up, and a chill went down my spine. I took a deep breath and a few moments to recover and said, 'Yes, darling, I'll be home early to have dinner with you Angelo and Mum and to blow out your birthday candles with you.'

What happened in the five minutes that followed, I cannot describe. It seemed to me like an hour. I was just standing there holding the phone, listening to them dancing and singing, 'Daddy is coming home early! Daddy is coming home early!'

My brain started ticking. It was then that I realised that what made my children happy didn't cost me anything and that I had been depriving them of it all this time. I realised that what was most important to them was me, their father, not the money and not the material things.

For the first time I realised that while we do need money to live, it was not the first priority, priority number one. I also understood what my wise wife meant when she said, 'What's the point of working if you can't spend time with your family?' Obviously, she is not a materialistic person and was satisfied with the simple things in life.

All these thoughts were going through my mind, driving all the way home, feeling guilty and wondering how I was going to face my kids. When I arrived, I parked my car in the driveway, picked up my briefcase, and walked up to the front door. But there was another surprise waiting that shook me. The front door was decorated with streamers and balloons, and a large sign that said: 'Welcome home, Daddy.' Believe it or not, I survived the heart attack this time as well, but I couldn't control my emotions. I sat on my briefcase, put my face in my palms, and bawled my eyes out. If that was meant to make me feel guilty, they had succeeded.

Christalene and Angelo saw me through the window. They opened the door and ran into my arms yelling, 'Daddy is home. Daddy is home.'

I was trying to wipe my tears when Christalene asked me, very sympathetically, 'Why are you crying, Daddy? Have we done something wrong?'

I looked at them and said, 'No, darling, you haven't done anything wrong. I am the one who wronged you.' They both looked at me puzzled wondering what I was talking about. It was then that I told them that I wanted to make them a promise. They asked what about and I said, 'As of today, I will never come home after six again. I will have dinner with you every night.'

Again they danced and sang and were very happy. That was the best present that I could give my children. I could clearly see it on their faces. It was like I gave them the world.

Christalene, Angelo, and Patch 1980

Well, I kept my promise, came home early every day, and spent time with them and took them to drama, soccer training, tennis, motorbike riding, and other sporting activities. I consider myself very lucky that my kids taught me this lesson on time, because kids cannot wait; they grow and leave home before we know it.

There is no doubt that your family is priority number one and, of course, they are the reasons for your working; you want to provide the best for them and you would be prepared to sacrifice a lot to achieve that, but be careful you don't get carried away in the process, like I did.

I write this trying to control my emotions, and I thank God that my kids taught me a lesson that changed my life.

4. *Avoolos noos, gamni din dihin yierimin.*
4. Αβουλος νους κάμνει την τύχην γέρημη.
4. Ill-considered actions bring misfortune.

Meaning
Ill-considered actions result in disaster and are looked upon as bad luck.

Used
Used when one's own foolish actions cause one misery and one blames one's luck when something goes wrong.

Example
Sitting on the Branch You Are Cutting

Zavos was a very clumsy and illogical man who was always complaining about his bad luck. Everything he did always went wrong, and he blamed his luck for it. One day he decided to go to the forest and chop some firewood. He saw a dead branch on a tree, so he climbed up with his hand saw.

As he was cutting it, an old man was passing by and made an observation.

He said to Zavos, 'When you finish cutting that branch up there you will fall down with it.'

Zavos looked at the old man, wondering how he could possibly know that, and without taking much notice of him, he proceeded with cutting the branch.

When he finished cutting the branch he, of course, fell down with it.

He got up swearing and blaming his luck as always; then he suddenly remembered the old man's words. He bolted after him, thinking that the old man had jinxed him and brought him the bad luck.

When he caught up with him, asked how he knew, he would fall down. The old man then replied, 'Because you were sitting on it while you were cutting it, you fool.'

Bappoo then said, '**A**voolos noos, **g**amni din **d**ihin **y**ierimin.'

Moral
Face reality and use logic to anticipate outcomes.

5. Avraon ambelin en doos yatharoos mandra.
5. Αβρανον αμπέλι εν τους γαδάρους μάντρα.
5. Open vineyard, donkey's stall.

Meaning
Those days there were many donkeys around, and if a vineyard was open, not fenced off to be protected, it would attract a lot of donkeys to chew up the vines.

Used
Used to advice one that it is necessary to take precautions to protect one's property in order to prevent damages or losses.

Example
James got a new job as a production manager in an aluminium window factory. The storeroom in which they kept the tools and

consumable hardware was always open, and the workers would walk in and help themselves as they pleased. James then put a lock on the door and appointed a storeman to control the stock. When he was asked why, he replied, '*Avraon ambelin en doos yatharoos mantra.*'

Moral
Prevention is better than cure.

6. Anayios don gollion na soo vgali da mmathkia soo.
6. Ανάγιως τον κολιόν να σου φκάλει τα μάθκια σου.
6. Bring up the jackdaw to poke your eyes out.

Meaning
You find a little *kolio* (a jackdaw) fallen out of its nest, you look after it, bring it up, and one day it pokes your eye out due to lack of loyalty.

Used
Used when children are inconsiderate and mistreat their parents.

Example
Kypro's Heartbreaking Story (True story)

Kypros migrated to Australia with his wife and two little boys in the early 1960s. He got a job at the wholesale fruit marked as a forklift driver, and for many years he worked very hard from three in the morning until late afternoon. During this time he had another two children, a boy and a girl, and he thought that it was time to step up and start his own business. He had saved enough money to open a little fruit shop. He knew the fruit in English by then, so nothing could stop him and off he went. The rest is history; the shop was doing well, but he was working seven days a week. He built a beautiful double-storeyed house, and he managed to send all his children to university to give them a sound education. By the time they graduated, he built them a double-storeyed house each and got them married.

His wife was by his side all along, but she wasn't feeling very well so he decided to pack up and retire at the age of seventy-two to enjoy what life he had left. Unfortunately, his wife was diagnosed with cancer, and not long after, she passed away. He was devastated, and his friends stood by him and encouraged him to go out to go to the Greek club and meet people, which he did and looked forward to it once a week. That helped him ease the pain for a while, and he started to enjoy life, until one day he went home and couldn't open the door. He sat on the front step and called one of his sons, who was an accountant. 'Son,' he said, 'I don't know what is wrong with the lock, but I can't open the front door.'

'Ah . . . Sorry, Dad,' he replied, 'but we all think that is time for you to go to the old people's home. The house is too big for you, and we think we should invest it in a more profitable way.' On hearing this, the poor man fainted, and Christo the neighbour called the ambulance.

When he opened his eyes on the hospital bed, he was crying and said, 'I can't believe what is happening. They made me transfer the title of my house on to their names, and now they want to take it away from me and throw me in a home, after all I have done for them? How low and ungratefull can they be.'

Bappoo then said, *'Anayios don gollion na soo vgali da mmathkia soo.'*

Moral
Respect and protect your parents.

7. Anaelasen ei eyia dis gooellas.
7. Αναέλασεν η αίγια της κουέλλας.
7. The goat mocked the sheep.

Christalene with her cousin Iakovo 1983

Meaning
The goat laughed and made fun of the sheep, forgetting her own shortcomings.

Used
Used when one with obvious deficiencies mocks one without.

Example
It's a funny story of a goat and a sheep playing in the field. As the sheep jumped over the fence, her tail lifted up exposing her bare bottom.

The goat then was in hysterics laughing at the sheep because she saw her bottom. The sheep then said to the goat, 'How can you laugh at me, when your bottom is permanently exposed?'

Bappoo said, *'An**a**elasen ei **e**yia dis goo**e**llas.'*

Moral
If you are not perfect, don't mock or criticise others.

If you mock or criticise others you are not perfect.

8. Aboo bellon je boo mitsin, na mathhis din alithkian.
8. Από πελλόν τζαι που μιτσήν να μάθεις την αλήθκειαν.
8. You learn the truth from a fool or a child.

Meaning
You are most likely to hear the truth from a foolish person or a child as they are both naïve and innocent and they don't know how to lie.

Used
Used when a child or a fool naively tells the truth.

Example
Alexandros to Spy on Dad (Joke)

Mummy had a suspicion for a while that Daddy was cheating on her because the bedroom smelt of a fragrance of a perfume she never used. She was trying to come to terms with it until one day she found a pair of undies under the bed which didn't belong to her. She was furious and decided to do something about it. The following morning she got little Alexandros ready before she went to work and said to him, 'Alexandros, you have a very important job to do today. You are not going to kinder today. I have an assignment for you.' He said, 'What's that, Mummy?' She replied, 'You will play the spy today. You will hide in the closet and wait until daddy comes home and see what he does, and when I come home lunchtime you let me know, OK?' 'OK, Mummy,' replied Alexandros. Lunchtime came and mommy came home. Alexandros ran to her all excited and said, 'Mummy, Mummy, I saw daddy come home with this blonde girl and...'

'OK,' mummy said, 'wait until after dinner when daddy is home.' She was not very happy about what she heard, but she tried to contain herself, did some shopping, then cooked as usual and waited until the husband came home. When they finished dinner she called Alexandros and said, 'Tell us what has happened today, big boy.'

'Today I was hiding in the closet, and I saw daddy come home with a blonde lady with large boobies.' The husband nearly choked on desert. He tried to say something mumbling, but mummy stopped him. 'Come on, Alexandros, tell us what you saw daddy doing.'

Then Alexandros stood up, took a deep breath, and said, 'I saw daddy doing to the blonde lady what the postman did to you in the shed, Mummy.'

Bappoo then said, '*Ab**oo** bell**on** je boo mitsin, na mathhis din alithkian.*'

Moral
Kids and the foolish are too naive to keep a secret.

> 9. *Aboo boni ba ston yiadron.*
> 9. Απού πονεί πα στο γιατρόν.
> 9. Who has the pain goes to the doctor.

Meaning
When you have a pain you go to the doctor yourself, you don't send others.

Used
Used when one expects others to do one's dirty work.

Example
My Mother-in-Law and I (True story)

When we arrived in Australia in 1977, my in-laws were kind enough to let us stay with them until we got on our feet. Eight months later we purchased our own house. I made a deal with the builder to buy it in a lock-up stage (unfinished interior), and this way I saved a lot of money. I worked in it between work and college and finished it myself, made the kitchen and all the furniture. Four months later we moved in, and everything was going fine. Irene would take the kids to school in the morning and I would pick them up after school. We worked as a team, and everything seemed tobe working fine. We had discussions about various issues and made decisions together.

A few months later, Irene started to change her mind on certain issues that we had agreed on, and one day as I was questioning her about it to get to the bottom of it she mentioned her mother. Then I thought, Aha . . . got it.

I asked Irene to call her parents and asked them to come over because I wanted to talk to them. Then I thought of what Bappoo said, *'Aboo boni ba ston yiadron,'* It means: Who has the pain goes to the doctor.

The next morning I called her to come over with my father-in-law because I wanted to have a chat with them. She sounded worried, but she said OK.

After work Irene cooked, and we all had dinner together. After dinner, my father-in-law asked what I wanted to talk about. My mother-in-law looked a bit worried, and I said, 'You are my father and you are my mother in Australia. I have a lot of respect for you, and I love you both. I want us to stay like this forever.'

They said, 'So do we.'

'Well,' I replied, 'in this case, I ask you to show me the same respect. Never come between my wife and myself.' My father-in-law was shaking his head, looking at his wife wondering what she did. I said then, 'When my wife and I make decisions and others interfere and change them behind my back, I am not happy. I want you to feel free to come to us both, any time, and give us your advice, and I want to feel free to come to you for an advice, but it is up to us to take it or not, and you have to respect that.'

To cut the long story short, they agreed to it, and we lived happily ever after. We never had an argument after that. For thirty-five years we had an amazing relationship, and they were a pleasure to be with.

Moral
Take control of your own affairs.

Find the root of the problem.

10. Abon 'appekso doo horoo, kseri bolla draoothgia.
10. Απόν αππέξω του χορού, ξέρει πολλά τραούθκια.
10. Who is not on the dance floor, knows all the songs.

Meaning
One is not actively involved in a matter and yet makes irresponsible comments.

Used
Used when one criticises and throws irresponsible comments from outside without having all the facts.

Example
In a club meeting, some members go around whispering into other members' ears about how things should be done, without knowing all the facts, but when they are asked to help or speak up, they have nothing to say or to offer. It's easier to sit back and criticise rather than doing something constructive.

Then Bappoo says, *'Ab**on** app**e**kso doo hor**oo**, kseri boll**a** dra**oo**thgia.'*

Moral
It is not constructive to criticise if you don't have all the facts.

11. Abon agooi doo yonioo, bara yonias jimade.
11. Απόν ακούει του γονιού, παραγωνιάς τζοιμάται.
11. Who doesn't take advice from parents ends up on the streets.

My mum and dad, Ioannis (Yannaros) and Christalleni Ioannou, 1987

Meaning
When one doesn't take advice from one's parents, there is every chance that one ends up on the streets.

It refers to cases where young people want to experience life on their own and like to exercise their judgement using the trial and error method, which is known to be the most costly method.

Used
Used when children are rebellious and don't like to be told by the parents what to do and learn the hard way.

Example
Steve was warned by his parents many times to get a job and to save money for his future, but he chose the easy and selfish way, sleeping in all day waiting for his parents to feed him, until one day they had enough and kicked him out. Then Bappoo said, 'A**bon** ag**oo**i doo yon**ioo**, bara yon**ia**s jim**a**de.'

Moral
Advice from parents can improve your quality of life.

This is a very popular proverb. It's advice to the young generation about how important it is to accept guidance from their parents, particularly during the developing years of their lives and on general everyday life matters that parents have experience in.

It doesn't mean, though, that one shouldn't ask questions. Many people do things in certain ways because they have been conditioned, particularly those with religious or cultural backgrounds, who have to go by 'the book', and quite often there is no logical explanation. I believe that we must allow the young ones to ask questions and give them facts, not answers like 'because that's how it has to be done' (Ma *etsi brebi*.) There are certain things that are passed on to us from past generations that don't apply to today's lifestyle, like the following story of grandma's Sunday roast.

Grandma's Sunday Roast

This is the story, I was told, of a little girl who was learning how to cook a Sunday roast. Her mumshowed her everything from start to finish then placed it in a dish, and before she put it in the oven, she cut the two ends with a sharp carving knife. The little girl very curiously asked her mum why she did that. Mum shrugged her shoulders and replied, 'I don't know, darling, that's how my mum taught me.'

So they went to see grandma in the granny flat at the rear of the house.

'Grandma, why did you cut the ends off the roast before you put it in the oven?' said the little girl. Grandma gave the same answer as mum, so they all went upstairs to ask the great-grandmother. She looked at them, smiled, and replied, 'In those days, sweetheart, the ovens were very small, and the roast couldn't fit in unless we cut the ends.'

Of course, now with such large ovens there is no need for that.

This is a clear indication that upbringing can play a very important role in one's behaviour and thinking. Parents that are open-minded and encourage their children to ask questions can avoid conditioning them to anything that doesn't apply to today's society.

12. Abo n'andrebete, o cosmos en'thikos doo.
12. Απόν αντρέπεται ο κόσμος εν δικός του.
12. Who feels no embarassement owns the world.

Meaning
He who doesn't feel embarrassment does what he likes, wherever he is, disregarding and disrespecting everything.

Used
Used when a person is not embarrassed, takes over, and shows no consideration for others, as if he owned the world.

Example
Stavros was invited to a friend's holiday house for the weekend and took his newcomer cousin Mimi with him. Mimi was so excited with the huge size of the house and all the conveniences that he went crazy. He rudely made himself at home, opened their fridge, used their bar, and lay on the couches with his shoes like he owned the place. The owners ignored him, but Stavros was so embarrassed that told him to pack up and go. Mimi looked at him wondering why and Stavros then said, '*Abon andrebede o gosmos en thigos doo.*'

Moral
Show respect and consideration to others.

13. Aboo varigoofa dergazi.
13. Από ύ βαρυκουφά, ταιρκάζει τα.
13. Who has hearing problem rhymes own words.

Meaning
If you have a hearing problem you make up verses that rhyme.

Used
When talking to one with hearing problem who makes up words that sound like the ones one heard.

Example
I said, 'A cow and a goat,' and he heard, 'A car on the road.' Bappoo says, '*Ab**oo** varigo**of**a derg**a**zi.*'

Moral
Pay more attention when conversing with people having hearing problems.

Bappoo (Grandpa) with the Hearing Aid (Joke)

Bappoo Stamatis was always sitting around quiet, watching the kids playing and kept out of everyone's way. He couldn't hear a thing anyway, and despite his wife's advice to do something about his hearing, he refused. After his wife passed away, his two daughters and three sons had a good talk with him about considering a hearing aid, because they needed to communicate. One day he got up took the bus and went to my friend George the audiologist for an assessment. A week later he was wearing a state-of-the-art in hearing aid. Everything was so tiny you couldn't tell that he was wearing it. He could hear the world again, and he was very happy about it. A month later he went back, as George advised him to do, for the final adjustment. George asked Bappoo Stamatis if his children were happy now that he could hear them. He replied, 'No, I haven't told them yet.' George was shocked with his answer and said, 'But why?' 'I sit around listening to their conversations quietly,' he replied. 'I changed my will two times already.'

14. Athkiaseros babas thhavki je doos zondanoos.
14. Αδκιασερός παπάς, θάφκει τζαι τους ζωντανούς.
14. Priest that's not busy buries people alive.

Meaning
A priest buries people alive when he is not busy just for the sake of having something to do.

Used
Used when one does unnecessary things simply because one has nothing else to do.

Example
Tex has recently retired;he had been active all his life, and he couldn't sit at home doing nothing. So he unnecessarily kept on stripping the paint on his house and re-painting it. Bappoo then said, '*Athgiaseros babas thhavki je doos zondanoos.*'

Moral
Use your time wisely.

15. Agooe bolla je bistevke llia.
15. Ακουε πολλά τζαι πίστευκε λλία.
15. Listen to a lot, believe a few.

Meaning
Listen to what people say, but don't believe everything you hear.

Used
It's used to express disbelief when one brags about something that one has heard or seen.

Example
Spiro is known to make up stories and put others down. One day we were talking about Johannesburg, and he rudely interrupted to say how beautiful a city it is. He said that he had the best time at the beach when he was there. I then sarcastically said, 'When I was in Johannesburg, the nearest beach was in Durban 600 km away.'

That's when Bappoo says, '*Agooe bolla je bistevke llia.*'

Moral
Don't believe everything you hear.

16. Alla loyia thhkie baba.
16. Άλλα λόγια θκε παπά.
16. Why the priest changed the subject.

Meaning
Traditionally, the priest of the village was the educated person that everyone went to for advice. When he was asked a question that he didn't like, or didn't have the answer for, he cleverly changed the subject.

Used
Used when one deliberately misleads you by changing the subject.

Example
The reporter asked the mayor of the town to explain what happened to the 35 million euros that was allocated for the construction of the town's sewerage network. He gave him a dirty look and said, 'It's the responsibility of the council to repair the football ground for this week's grand finale.'

'Yes, sir, but what about the 35 million euros for the sewer?'

'As a responsible mayor I can assure you that all proceeds from the game will go to the senior citizens home.'

The reporter then laughed and said, *'Alla loyia thhkie baba.'*

Moral
Stay in control when you ask questions.

17. Allaksen o Manolios, J'evalen da rooha doo alios.
17. Αλλαξεν ο Μανωλιός τζ' έβαλεν τα ρούχα του αλλοιώς.
17. Manuel dressed differently now.

Meaning
Manuel has changed the way he dresses to fool people, but inside he is still Manuel.

Used
Used when one changes appearance or attitude to mislead another.

Example
Manolios was a mean man known in the village for his tendencies to drink and annoy others in the *cafenio* (coffee shop). Even when he was sober he mocked and made fun of others. They tried to avoid him as much as they could to enjoy a drink in peace, but wherever they went there he was.

One day he was reading a notice on the noticeboard regarding the forthcoming council elections. He stopped and thought for a minute and with a big smile on his face went home to his wife. 'Darling,' he said, 'I have an idea. I will run for the council at the next elections.' On hearing the word 'darling', she was shocked because he had never called her darling before.

He then said that he would need her support. The following Sunday after church, he was first at the cafenio waiting by the front door, and as the people came in, very politely he greeted every one of them and showed unusual kindness. Everyone was wondering what happened to Manolios and why the change until his wife told them that he decided to become a politician. Bappoo then said, *'**A**llaksen o Manoli**os**, J'**e**valen da r**oo**ha doo ali**os**.'*

Moral
Don't be fooled by appearance.

18. Alla enda mmathkia doo laoo, jalla doo gookkoofkiaoo.
18. Άλλα εν τα μμάθκια του λαού τζι άλλα του κουκκουφκιάου.
18. The eyes of the owl are one thing, and
the eyes of the hare another.

Meaning
There is no comparison between the eyes of a hare with those of an owl.

The owl has a 70-degree binocular vision, and the large size of its eyes enables it to see in the dark.

Used
Used to highlight the superiority of an item with an inferior one.

Example
I went to buy a BMW motor car. We had a look around, checked some different cars, and when the sales man gave us the price I said, 'How is it that the X Japanese car is so much cheaper?'

The sales man then got offended, saying, 'How can you compare a BMW with the X? *Alla enda mmathkia doo laoo je alla doo gookkoofkiaoo*'

Moral
Don't compare something of superior quality with an inferior option.

19. Alli spernoon je thherizoon, Jalli dron je voortoonizoon.
19. Άλλοι σπέρνουν τζαι θερίζουν τζι
άλλοι τρων τζαι βουρτουνίζουν.
19. Some do the sowing and harvesting,
and others get the crop.

Meaning
The people who have done all the work don't get any benefit, and others who have done nothing reap the benefits.

Used
When one unjustly reaps the benefit or takes credit for what others have done.

Example
My friend Christo past away recently after a long battle with dementia. Of course, with long illness like this you need a full-time carerer, and in this case the daughter put her own life on hold to provide that care. Fifteen years she looked after her father, giving him lots of love and attention. The oldest brother

never showed any interest at all until Christo died. He then went to the lawyers claiming his father's little house. He was a very shrewd man and somehow he managed to put it on his name. The poor sister was left with nothing. Bappoo then said, *'Alli spernoon je thherizoon, Jalli dron je magarizoon.'*

Moral
It's not fair to take what's not yours.

20. Ama thipsa i avli soo, men shienonnis do neron se ksenes avles.
20. Αμα διψά η αυλή σου, μεν σιονώννεις
το νερό σε ξένες αυλές.
20. If your garden is dry, don't pour water on other gardens.

Meaning
When one attends to problems of others and neglects one's own.

Used
When one places the interest of others ahead of one's own.

Example
Odyssas's wife was complaining about her husband, spending all his free time doing favours for everybody else, when his own house was falling apart and needed so much attention. Bappoo then said, '*Ama thipsa i avli soo, men shienonnis do neron se ksenes avles.*'

Moral
Your family comes first.

21. Ammen lathkiasis don drohon, en yirizi.
21. Αμμέν λαθκιάσεις τον τροχόν, εν γυρίζει.
21. The wheel will not turn if you don't lubricate it.

Meaning
If you want the wheel to keep turning, it is necessary that you lubricate it regularly.

Used
It's a statement used to express the importance of giving incentives to employees or others, in order to achieve higher productivity.

In many cases it is used to buy off government officials, and of course that is bribery and is illegal.

Bribery is defined by *Black's Law Dictionary* as the offering, giving, receiving, or soliciting of any item of value to influence the actions of an official or the person in charge of a public or legal duty.

Example

Peter employed a gardener to mow his lawn. When he asked him to remove some rubbish that he had behind the shed the gardener hesitated, saying that he was not a cleaner. Then Peter offered him more money, and the job was done. Bappoo says, *'Ammen lathkiasis don drohon, en yirizi.'*

Moral

Incentives increase performance and productivity.

The Dog's Funeral (Joke)

A man walked into a church with a dead dog in his arms. He went up to the priest and asked him kindly if he could do a burial service for his dog.

The priest gave him a dirty look and replied angrily, 'How dare you bring an animal into the house of God?'

He then said, 'But, Father, this dog has been a member of my family for fifteen years.'

This made the priest a little sympathetic and he said calmly, 'Take your dog down to the end of the street. There is an Anglican church there. They love animals, and I am sure if you give them a small donation they will bury him for you.'

'Ah, thank you, Father!' he replied gratefully.

As he was exiting the church, he turned around and asked the priest if he thought 10,000 dollars would be a sufficient donation.

Hearing this, the priest's eyes popped out. He came over and ushered the man back in.

'Come here, my dear son. Why didn't you tell me your dog is Orthodox?'

> *22. Ama en bai o Moamethh sto voonon,*
> *bai do voonon is don Moamethh.*
>
> 22. Αμαν εν πάει ο Μωάμεθ στο βουνό,
> πάει το βουνό στον Μωάμεθ.
>
> 22. If Mohammad doesn't go to the mountain,
> the mountain goes to Mohammad.

Meaning

Mohammad has to go to the mountain to pray, regardless of what happens. When is time to pray if he is unable to go, he would still pray as if he was on the mountain.

Used

Used when one is unable to do something or be somewhere and improvises.

Example

I repeatedly asked my brother-in-law to bring me his chain, saw to cut some branches off my tree and he kept on saying OK, but it never eventuated. One day I went to his house and picked it up myself. He was very apologetic for not been able to bring it, so I said to him, 'Don't worry. *Ama en bai o Moamethh sto voonon, bai do voonon is don Moamethh.*'

Moral

Improvise.

23. An ekseres din bedran boo idan na goodsoovlisis, eboirizes din.
23. Αν έξερες την πέτραν πούταν να κουτσουβλίσεις, επογύριζες την.
23. If you knew the stone you would trip on, you would have avoided it.

Meaning
If you could anticipate the problem, you would have prevented it.

Used
To show moral support to one that had a freak accident or misfortune.

Example
Harry was going olive picking one morning on horseback. The horse saw a snake crossing its path and bolted down the hill. Harry lost his balance and fell off the horse and ended up in the

hospital. Many friends went to visit him, and his wife then said, *'An ekseres din bedran boo idan na goodsoovlisis, eboirizes din.'*

Moral
Freak accidents can happen to anyone.

24. Abo n'imbori na theri don yaron, thernni do saman.
24. Απόν ημπορεί να δέρει τον γάρον, δέρνει το σάμα.
24. Who can't hit the donkey hits the saddle.

English version: Who can't kill the king kills the messenger.

Meaning
One take's out one's anger on the wrong people, because they don't have the guts, the ability, or the courage to punish the ones responsible.

Used
Used when one is weak to face and deal with a problem and is going about it the wrong way.

Example
The managing director of a company told his manager that he will not get bonus this quarter because sales have not reached targets. The manager was furious and took it out on other employees in the office.

That's when Bappo says, 'Who can't beat the donkey beats the saddle – *Abo n'imbori na theri don yaron, thernni do saman.*'

Moral
Deal with the cause of a problem.

25. Aboshi thendron, eshi oshion ja boshi oshion jimate.
25. Απόσιει δέντρον έσιει οσσιόν τζαι αποσιει οσσιον τζοιματε.
25. Who has a tree has shade, and who has shade sleeps

Meaning
People with children, relatives, or friends that can be relied upon in the event of need can rest.

Used
Used when one in need has someone to rely on.

Example
Angela, a seventy-year-old lady, has five children and many friends, and when she needs something; there is always someone there for her.

That's when Bappoo says, *'Aboshi thendron, eshi oshion ja boshi oshion jimate.'*

Moral

Having children and good friends to rely on is a blessing.

26. Abon eshi noon, eshi bothgia.
26. Απόνεσιει νουν, έσιει πόδκια.
26. Who doesn't think walks.

Cairns, Australia

Meaning
Your careless or thoughtless actions waste time and effort.

Used
Used when one is thoughtless and either does things twice or uses the wrong, long method.

Example
Spiro wanted to fill up his new swimming pool with water. He was using a bucket and filling it from the nearest tap. His father

saw him and said, 'Why don't you use a hose? *Ab*o*n eshi n*oo*n e*shi b*o*thgia.'

Moral

There is always a better and cheaper way of doing something; you just have to think and find it.

27. *Abo shi mooyian, mooyiazete.*
27. Απόσιει μούγιαν, μουγιάζεται.
27. Who has a fly gets annoyed.

English version: He has a chip on his shoulder.

Meaning
One's defensive reaction gives away one's guilt when a subject is brought up.

Used
Used when one reacts defensively on hearing others talking about a subject that can incriminate or expose one.

Example
I was talking about Gamblers Anonymous with some friends one day, and Spiro's wife got defensive and told me to mind my own business, because it was her money she gambled and she could

do what she liked with her money. I replied that I had no idea she gambled, but it showed that as Bappoo says, *'Abo shi mooyian, mooyiazete.'*

Moral

Your reactions can often expose you.

28. Arhi horis delos, anofeli.
28. Αρχή χωρίς τέλος, ανώφελη.
28. Beginning without end is pointless.

Ora's primary school

Meaning
There is no benefit when you start something and do not finish it.

Used
When one starts many things but never gets to finish any.

Example
Spiro is very good with his hands and has a lot of good ideas.

He gets overexcited when he thinks of an idea, starts putting it into practice, but eventually loses interest for one reason or another and doesn't get to finish anything.

That's when Bappoo says, '*Arhi horis delos, anofeli.*'

Moral
To finish is more important than to start.

29. Akooe meyalon thendron, je berne mitsin galathin.
29. Άκου μεγάλο δέντρον τζι έπερνε μιτζίν καλάθι.
29. When you hear of a large tree, take a small basket.

Ironically, this is probably the largest eggplant tree you have ever seen.
Just for comparison purposes, my fence next to it is 1.5 metres high.
It is my ten-year-old melinzana tree (eggplant) in my backyard.
It has been crafted on a dragon plant (like a rose bush) and is under cover.
It produces over a 1,000 eggplants per year during the summer months.
(True story)

Meaning
When you hear of a large tree, you automatically assume that there will be a lot of fruit to be picked and you take a large basket. Don't always believe it because people exaggerate.

Used
Used when one exaggerates or brags.

Example
The West Gate Bridge (Joke)

I went to the airport to pick up a potential supplier from Texas. All the way to the hotel he didn't stopped talking and kept bragging about how big things are in Texas. He looked at the Tullamarine freeway and said, 'Look how small your roads are in Australia. They are not as big as our freeways in Texas.'

After a few minutes, looking down at the bay he commented on how small it was, not as big as his swimming pool. Then going over the bridge, he laughed at the small size of it. He said, 'The bridge over my pond in my front yard is larger than this one.'

As we were halfway to Geelong, we saw two kangaroos hopping across the freeway at high speed. I then looked at him and exclaimed, 'Bloody grasshoppers, they are everywhere!'

Moral
Don't believe everything you hear.

> *30. Alli psihomahoon, je alli gavlomahoon.*
> 30. Άλλοι ψυχομαχούν τζι άλλοι καβλομαχούν.
> 30. Some are dying, and others want sex.

Meaning
While some are suffering, others worry about their self-indulgence.

Used
When inconsiderate people don't care when others are going through a crisis or rough times and only worry about themselves.

Example
During a fire everyone was rushing out of the house to survive. A lady next door complained to the firemen that they made a mess in her driveway. The fireman said, '*Alli psihomah**oo**n, je alli gavlomah**oo**n.*'

Moral
Show compassion in other's misfortune.

31. Astia, astia, ma aggastrothika.
31. Αστεία Αστεία, μα αγγαστρωθηκα.
31. Joking, joking, but I got pregnant.

Meaning
There are certain things that you can't joke about.

Used
Used when one goes too far with offending jokes that are disrespectful or even harmful.

Example
The Pregnant Girl

Spiro met a girl out in the field. She was quite naive and he tried to take advantage of her. He asked her to play a game, just for a joke, and she said okay. He then asked her to take her dress off, and she obliged. Then he said, 'Can you remove your underwear?' On hearing that, she pulled back and looked at him suspiciously and said no way. He insisted, saying that there was nothing to worry about because it was only for a joke.

She thought about it for a minute and said, 'Okay if it's for a joke, I'll do it,' and proceeded to take her underwear off. He then went closer and commenced having sex with her. At this point she said to him, 'You keep saying it's a joke, it's a joke, but for a joke you got me pregnant.'

Bappoo then said, *'Astia, astia, ma aggastrothika.'*

Moral
Be discreet with jokes as they may offend some.

32. Ama eshis dethkioos filoos, inda thelis doos ohtroos.
32. Αμαν έσιεις τέθκιους φίλους, ήντα θέλεις τους οχτρούς.
32. With friends like these, you don't need enemies.

Meaning
You don't need friends that hurt you like enemies do.

Used
It's used to express your hurt and disappointment when a friend betrays you.

Example
My friend Alex borrowed my truck to help his son move house. He knocked the neighbours' fence down, and he didn't mention anything. Two weeks later I received a letter from a solicitor to pay $3,400 plus expenses for the gate with a photograph of my truck attached. I checked the rear bumper bar of the truck and saw the marks. When I confronted him, he denied any involvement, and I had to pay the damage. Bappoo then said, '*Ama eshis dethkioos filoos, inda thelis doos ohtroos.*'

Moral
Choose your friends wisely.

33. Ama miniskis se yiallenon spidin, men bedassis betres.
33. Αν μεινίσκεις σε γυάλλενο σπίτι, μεν πετάσσεις πέτρες.
33. If you live in a glass house, don't throw stones.

Meaning

If you live in a glass house, you mustn't throw stones, because that will provoke others to throw stones back at you.

Used

Used when one with many faults or bad reputation dares to criticise others.

Example

Noni has two sons. One is in jail and the other is wanted by the police for rape and robbery. I saw her at the market the other day, and she was bad-mouthing my friend's daughter. Then I said to her, '*Ama miniskis se yiallenon spidin, men bedassis betres.*'

Moral

Consider your shortcomings before you criticise others.

34. Ama this din goofin, men yirevkis din golosirmathkian dis.
34. Άμα δεις τήν κουφή μέ γυρεύκεις την κωλοσυρμαθκιάν της.
34. If you see the snake, don't look for its trail.

Meaning
If you see the snake, why would you be looking for its trail?

Used
When you know where the problem is and you hesitate to solve it because you don't want to face reality for one reason or another.

Example
In the local town council money was went missing from the cash register quite often. They caught the thief red-handed, but the policeman still wanted to conduct an investigation to confirm that money was actually missing.

Bappoo then said, *'Ama this din goofin, men yirevkis din golosirmathkian dis.'*

Moral
Face reality and take action.

35. Amm'en glapsi do moron, i mana en do daizi.

35. Αμμέν κλάψει το μωρό, η μάνα εν το ταΐζει.

35. If the baby doesn't cry, its mother won't feed it.

Christalene with her first baby,
Angelo, Maryland, USA, 2010

Meaning

Even a mother won't feed her baby if it doesn't cry.

Used

To stress the importance of communication in order to achieve a goal.

Example

We had a new worker, and I noticed that he was holding his head at one stage. I approached him and asked if there was anything wrong. He then said, 'Yes, I have a terrible headache, but there is no first aid box.' So I sent him to the chemist and organised a full first aid box and set it up in a little room. He thanked me and said, 'It's good to have it.'

Bappoo then said, *'Amm'en glapsi do moron, i mana en do daizi.'*

Moral
Communicate for your needs and demand your rights.

36. Amm'en ispiris, en thherizis.
36. Αμμέν ησπύρεις εν θερίζεις.
36. If you don't sow, you don't reap.

Meaning
If you don't put in the work, you can't get the benefit.

Used
Used when one has expectations and demands, without contribution.

Moral
Contribute to have benefits.

Example
Aesop's Fable: The Ant and the Grasshopper

Ants are known to be hard-working and community-orientated little creatures. They are very good at planning and working together as a team, and I think we have a lot to learn from them.

Once there was an ant carrying a huge grain of wheat on its back.

A grasshopper was outside hopping, playing around, and singing. He then asked the ant to go and play with him, but the ant replied that he had to work now, as the weather was good, to stock up food for winter.

The grasshopper continued to play and said, 'You stupid ant, I will play all summer and enjoy myself, and you will spend it working, ha-ha!'

Winter came and the hard-working ant's storerooms were full. All the ants were dancing and singing with full stomachs in their warm ant kingdom, and they didn't have to worry about going out in the cold.

The grasshopper, on the other hand, had no food stored, so he had to go out in the freezing cold and search for it.

It was very difficult for him to move as his legs were frozen and also, everything was snowed under and he couldn't find any food to eat. A few days went by and he was so weak that he couldn't stand on his feet. Eventually he collapsed to the ground and died.

The ant took a peek, saw the grasshopper dead, and said, 'You stupid grasshopper! *Amm'en ispiris en thherizis.*'

Moral
Contribute to have benefits.

37. Athe befkoos yia ilarka.
37. Αδε πεύκους για υλάρκα.
37. These pine trees are good for sieve rings.

Meaning
These trees have such a good and flexible wood that it can make beautiful rings for sieves (a comment expected from a tradesman).

Used
Used when one of high position makes comments to show one's low status (perhaps promoted without proper qualifications).

Example
The Sieve Maker (Mantis) That Became a King

A villager once dressed up as a gentleman, went into town, and became a king. One day as he was going through the woods with his company, he looked at some very straight pine trees and said, 'Oh, my God, these pines would make excellent sieve rings. *Athe befkoos yia ilarka.*'

That's how he dobbed himself in that he was a tradesman. He couldn't help thinking like one, even when he became a king. Everyone then realised that he was a village tradesman that had no royal blood in him. He was ridiculed, laughed at, and chased away.

Moral
Don't try to be someone you are not qualified to be.

*38. Aboo ssothgiazi endega je boo ksothgiazi thega,
en athrobos doo hairgoo je thosde doo yienegan.*
38. Από σωδκιάζει έντεκα τζι από ξοδκιάζει δέκα.
Εν άθρωπος του χαϊρκού τζαι δώστε του γεναίκα.
38. He who spends less than he earns
prospers and deserves a wife.

Meaning
If you spend less than what you earn, you are a good money manager; you will prosper and easily find a wife.

Used
Used to show the importance of being a good money manager and also increase your chances of finding a wife.

Example
The Bucket with a Hole (True story)

I remember when my son Angelo was still in the last years of elementary school, we had a discussion about economics and how to save money as he had a tendency to spend. I asked him how he would solve the following problem. 'If I give you a bucket that had a hole at the bottom and asked you to fill it up with water, under a tap that runs in at five litres per minute and runs out at six litres per minute, how long do you think it would take the bucket to fill up?'

He laughed and said, 'Never.'

Then I asked him whether he had a solution for the problem and he replied, 'Yes, very easy, open the tap full to have more going in than coming out.'

Then I laughed and said, 'That's the hard way. The most logical way of solving this problem is to control the water that's going out of the bucket. Obviously your standards are too high, and I hope when you grow up, you make a lot of money and even so, when you spend more than you earn, your "bucket will always be empty".' He looked at me and nodded his head.

Moral
Spend less than you earn to prosper.

Marriage by Proxy

Most married couples used to meet, in those days, by proxy.

The proxy person (*broxenitra*) had a very important task, not only to bring them together but also to decide who was suitable for whom as she knew everybody in the village and knew who would be the best match. It was very important, as it is now, for the prospective husband to be a hard-working person and a good money-manager.

Of course, they had to meet other criteria as well, and if they had a bad reputation, it would be extremely difficult for them to find a spouse from that region.

This proverb is also used to emphasise to the offspring how important it is to be good money-managers. It doesn't matter how much money you make; if you spend more than what you earn, you will always be in debt.

> *39. Allin mas ethiksen je allin mas embiksen.*
> 39. Αλλην μας έδειξεν τζι άλλην μας έμπηξεν.
> 39. He showed us one and pricked us with another.

Meaning
One showed us one thing and delivered another.

Used
Used when one promises one thing and does another.

Example
I took up a travel insurance policy and mentioned to the salesman what our requirements were, and he tailored the policy to suit our needs.

My wife subsequently had a little health scare and spent a couple of days in the hospital in Annapolis for certain tests. When we came back and lodged a claim, we were told that she was not covered. That's when I said, '*Allin mas ethiksen je allin mas embiksen.*'

Moral
Beware of dishonest salespeople and read the fine print.

40. Andan na psorkasi o yidos sou, je soo votanin yirevke,
40. Αμαν ψωρκάσει ο γείτος σου, τζ' εσού βοτάνι γύρευκε.
40 When your neighbour catches scab, look for a remedy too.

Meaning
If your neighbour gets scab, it's most likely to spread to you too, and you must act immediately to prevent it from spreading.

Used
Used as a prevention warning when you see something coming.

Example
I was talking with my next-door neighbour, and he told me that his water bill had gone up dramatically. When I went inside, I said to my wife that we had to reduce our water usage. She said, 'What brought that up?'

I replied, *'Andan na psorkasi o yidos sou, je soo votanin yirevke.'*

Moral
Prevention is better than cure.

41. Ab'ayaba, bethevki.
41. Απ'αγαπά πεδεύκει.
41. He who cares for you counsels you.

Anastasia 2, Angelo 5, and Bappoo Jimmy in Annapolis, USA, 2014

Meaning
It's similar to 'Be cruel to be kind'. When parents are in the process of teaching the children the good from the bad and the right from wrong, arguments may erupt. The children often object to certain things, which put the parents in a dilemma to choose between compromising their kids' safety and welfare with their friendship.

Used
Used when you have to compromise your children's friendship to discipline them.

Example
The Egg Thief

Many years ago, the execution of criminals by hanging not only was socially accepted but was a regular occurrence in the town centre square.

One day a notorious thief was to be hanged, and everyone in the town had gathered around to watch. Before the judge gave the signal to pull the pin, they asked the man if he had a last wish. He nodded yes, and the judge approached him to hear his request.

I would like to kiss my mother, he said with a tear running down his cheek. They called his mother up on the stand, and when she leant over, much to the crowd's amazement, he bit her ear off.

When the guards took her away, the judge asked the obvious question. 'Why? Why did you do that?'

After a few minutes of silence he replied, 'When I was a little four-year-old boy, I was playing outside one day near the neighbour's chicken house, and I saw an egg lying in the corner inside the hen house. I sneaked my hand through the chicken wire, picked it up, and took it to my mother feeling very proud of my achievement. She took it, praised me for it, and then cooked it for me. Feeling very proud, the following day I took two eggs, then a dozen, then eventually a chicken, then a bank, and twenty years later, here I am a professional thief.'

You can't always blame the parents for their adult children's actions, but in this case, the mother not only didn't teach her child from day one that stealing is wrong, but she actually encouraged him by cooking the eggs.

This was his first step to becoming a thief at the age of four. If the mother had told him that what he did was stealing and that stealing was wrong and sent him to take the egg back where he found it, I am sure that this child would have stopped stealing there and then.

It is the parent's responsibility to teach and discipline little kids. They love exploring and picking up things that don't belong to them, and if parents don't teach them there and then, who will? It is much easier to do it at the earliest possible age. The older they get, the harder it becomes. Kids need boundaries, but we must be very careful not to confuse punishment with violent behaviour. We must be firm but gentle.

Moral
Kids don't need forty-year-old friends. They need parents to discipline them and give them boundaries. They need parents to show them the right road.

King Solomon once said, 'Teach the child from the first step of his road, and he will not depart from it.'

Greek: Διδαξον το παιδιον, εν αρχη της οδου αυτου και ουκ θελει απελθει απ αυτης εως οτου γηρασει.

42. Aryia midir basis kakias.
42. Αργία, μήτηρ πάσης κακίας.
42. Lazing idle is mother of all evil.

Meaning
If you don't work, you will be broke and bored. That would most likely cause unhappiness and all sorts of other problems.

Used
Used to emphasise the importance of keeping oneself occupied.

Example
When you work you make money and you pay your bills and your mortgage and buy whatever you like. This keeps you happy and secure, but money is not the most important benefit you get out of working. The most important benefit is *occupational therapy*, something that not many lazy people take into consideration, nor do they understand its value.

If you don't work, you get bored; boredom could cause unhappiness, depression, and other mental illness which, combined with lack of money, is a recipe for disaster. That could lead to all sorts of bad habits and illegal activities.

Moral
Work is important for your sanity, well-being, and financial independence.

43. Agapa don filon sou, me da elattomada doo.
43. Αγάπα τον φίλο σου με τα ελαττώματα του.
43. Love your friend with his faults.

Meaning
You must love your friend even if he/she has faults.

Used
Usually used after a quarrel between friends.

Example
Johnnie and I had a discussion regarding a problem he had with Kevin, one of his best friends. He said that Kevin had a heart of gold, but when they went out, he couldn't control himself after he had a few drinks and would cause arguments. I said to him, 'Make sure you keep an eye on him and talk to him about controlling his drinking, as we all have faults.'

Moral
Accept your friends for who they are.

44. Abon d'areskoon i sfirkes, en ba ston goomothromon.
44. Απόν τ' αρέσκουν οι σφυρκές, εν πα στον κωμοδρόμο.
44. Who doesn't like hammering, doesn't go to the blacksmith.

Similar to the English version:
If you can't take the heat, get out of the kitchen.

Meaning
You know there is hammering at the blacksmith. If you don't like it, you shouldn't go there.

Used
Used when one is aware of what one gets into and still does it and gets into trouble.

The sixth of January is the day of Thheophania and is an important day for Christianity, particularly the Greek Orthodox.

It is customary for the priest to throw a cross in the water from the pier, symbolising the baptism of Jesus. Many gutsy young men volunteer to dive in the freezing water to retrieve the cross in order to get the blessings. Fethonis was one of the young men that volunteered to dive despite the fact that he hated cold water and was susceptible to cold. Of course, he caught pneumonia and ended up in a hospital for treatment. Then Bappoo said, '*Abon d'areskoon i sfirkes, en ba ston goomothromo*'

Moral
Avoid things that can do you harm.

45. Akoma en don ithamen je Yiannin don evkalamen.
45. Ακόμα εν τον είδαμε τζαι Γιάννην τον εφκάλαμε.
45. We called him Yianni before we even saw him.

Similar to the English version:
Don't count your chickens before they hatch.

Meaning
The baby was not born yet, and we gave him a boy's name based on the assumption that it would be a boy.

Used
Used when one rushes to make a decision based on assumptions.

Example
Zavos planted tomatoes in his farm for the first time. He was making plans what he would do with them. He decided to use half of them for sauce and half to sell fresh; then he said he would buy himself a new car. His wife said, '*Akoma en don ithamen je Yiannin don evkalamen,*' because the weather was not getting any hotter and the frost could destroy the crop.

Moral
Never assume anything.

46. Ashimofore, je men rias.
46. Ασσιημοφόρε τζαι μεν ριάς.
46. Dress badly and be warm.

Meaning
If you don't have a choice, it's better to dress warmly than worry about style.

Used
Used to stress the importance of keeping yourself warm rather than look good.

Example
I saw a homeless person in a park one cold evening and offered him a blanket to keep warm He looked at it and didn't accept it because he didn't like the colour. I then said, '*Ashimofore, je men rias.*'

Moral
In the cold warmth is more important than looks.

47. Athrobos ayrammados, ksilon abelejidon.
47. Άδρωπος αγράμματος, ξύλον απελέτζητον.
47. Uneducated person uncarvable hard wood.

Meaning
It is very hard to get through to an uneducated person, like trying to carve a very hard wood.

Used
Used when you can't get through to one due to lack of education, understanding, and stubbornness.

Example
Zavos went to the post office to post a parcel. He walked in, and ignoring the long queue, he walked to the counter and asked for service. A gentleman behind me asked him to join the queue, but Zavos ignored him. The lady behind the counter said politely that he had to wait for his turn. Zavos then yelled that he was in a hurry and didn't care, and he demanded to be served. The manager then called security, who took him out. That is when Bappoo says, '*Athrobos ayrammados, ksilon abelejidon.*'

Moral
Don't argue with uneducated people that are very argumentative and stubborn and think they know it all.

*48. Aboo berna je ellali meyiasoo megalos don, sto
panairin ebardon jeosa soo thosoon thos don.*
48. Απου περνα τζιαι εν λαλει με γεια σου με καλως τον,
στο παναηριν επαρτον τζαι οσα σου δωσουν δως τον.
48. The person who doesn't greet take him to the
market and sell him for as little as you get.

Meaning
If you don't greet when you meet others, it is an indication of disrespect and you are not considered to be polite, sociable, or friendly (usually in small communities that know each other).

Used
Used when one meets an acquaintance and doesn't acknowledge them by greeting (say *'Yia sas'*).

Example

We were seating at a cafenio (coffee shop) in the village enjoying the sun and a cup of Greek coffee with some friends. While we were playing a game of *tavli* (back gammon) Nikoli walked past without saying anything or even looking our way. At that moment Bappoo Harry said, '*A**b**oo* *b**er**n**a* *je* *e**ll**a**l**i* *m**ey**ia**s**oo* *m**eg**al**os* *d**on*, *sto panairin e**b**a**r**do**n* *j**e**o**s**a* *soo* *th**o**s**oon* *th**os* *don.*'

Moral

It's polite to greet an acquaintance when you meet him/her.

49. Aboshi thendron, eshi oshion ja boshi oshion jimate.
49. Απόσιει δέντρον έσιει οσσιόν τζαι αποσιει οσσιον τζοιματε.
49. Who has a tree has shade, and who has shade sleeps.

Meaning
People with children, relatives, or friends that can be relied upon in the event of need can rest.

Used
Used when one in need has someone to rely on.

Example
Angela, a seventy-year-old lady has five children and many friends and when she needs something, there is always someone there for her.

That's when Bappoo says, *'Ab**o**shi thendron, **e**shi oshi**o**n ja b**o**shi oshi**o**n jim**a**te.'*

Moral
Having children and good friends to rely on is a blessing.

B

1. Ban medron ariston (from the Greek philosopher, Diogenes Laertius).
1. Παν μέτρον άριστον.
1. Everything in moderation.

Meaning
Too much of anything could be bad for you. Whatever we do, eat, drink work, etc., it's okay as long as we don't overdo it.

Used
Used when people overdo something or exceed their limitations.

Example
My father was one of the rangers of the village (ayrofilakas). His duty was to look after the fields, crops, and trees in the area and protect them from animals that ran loose. My mother used to pack his traditional backpack, called *voorka*, with his lunch. He would hide it somewhere in the area so he wouldn't have to carry it and then pick it up at lunchtime. One day he hid it in a narrow hollow of an olive tree trunk to keep it cool and also to protect it from predators. When he returned to pick up his lunch he was stunned to see a fox trying to squeeze out of that hollow, unable to move as it was stuck in there. Going in with empty stomach was easy, but coming out with an overfull stomach was impossible.

Then Bappoo said, '*Ban medron ariston.*'

Moral
Everything in moderation.

2. Bes moo me bioos bas, na soo bo bios ise.
2. Πες μου με ποιούς πας, να σου πω ποιός εισαι.
2. Tell me who your friends are, and I'll tell you who you are.

Meaning

Your friends can play a very important role in your reputation.

Used

It's used to emphasise the importance of choosing one's friends.

Example

My mother always told me to choose my friends carefully and that it was very important that they were good people. 'It's like fresh potatoes in a hessian bag. If there is one rotten potato in that bag, then in no time the whole bag will rot.'

If you mix with thieves you are likely to be treated like one; if you mix with gentlemen you are more likely to be one.

Bappoo said, *'Bes moo me bioos bas, na soo bo bios ise.'*

Moral

Choose your friends wisely if you value your reputation.

3. Bera vreshi, stin Garamanian shionizi.
3. Πέρα βρέσιει, στην Καραμανιά σιονίζει.
3. It's raining overseas and snowing on Mount Karamania (in Turkey).

Meaning
The person you are talking to is preoccupied and not paying any attention.

Used
Used when you talk to one that doesn't pay any attention because one's mind is far away.

Example
The manager of the hotel was briefing the staff about an important guest's arrival at the hotel and noticed one was yawning and not paying any attention. He gave him a look and said, *'Bera vreshi, stin Garamanian shionizi.'*

Moral
Get one's attention prior to talking.

4. Bebse don bellon, je lamne dabison doo.
4. Πέψε τον πελλόν τζαι λάμνε ταπισόν του.
4. Send a fool and go after him.

Meaning
If you send an idiot to do something you have to go after him to redo it yourself.

Used
Used when you wrongly allocate work to unqualified people and they stuff up.

Example
Paul had employed unqualified workers that were ignorant, and anything he asked them to do, he had to do it again himself. The last time I saw it happen, I said to him, 'Remember what Bappoo said, *"Bebse don bellon, je lamne dabison doo."'*

Moral
Delegate work to one that's capable or qualified.

5. Belloo J'ayioo, men daksis.
5. Πελλού τζ' αγίου μεν τάξεις.
5. Do not promise a fool or a saint.

Meaning
A fool or a saint has a good memory when you promise them something, and they will pester you until you fulfil your promise.

Used
It's used when one keeps bothering you to fulfil a promise you made.

Example
Spiro promised Hulk the madman that he would find him a wife, and ever since he is at Spiro's doorstep every morning asking if he did.

Bappoo then said to him, '*Belloo Je ayioo, men daksis.*'

Moral
If you don't want any headaches, don't promise anything to a fool or a saint.

6. *Bernise stin vrisin, Je fernise abodon.*
6. Πέρνει σε στη βρύση τζιαι φέρνει σε άποτον.
6. Takes you to the fountain and brings you back thirsty.

Meaning

A sweet-talker can take you to the water fountain and keep you so interested in what he says that you forget to drink and come back thirsty.

Used

Used when one is manipulative and smooth-talks you into following one's recommendations.

Example

Yiorgi the Sales Man

Yiorgi was a salesman on his first day in one of those superstores that sell everything from needles to kit homes. The manager called him upstairs, at the end of his shift, to explain why he only made one sale all day. He said, 'Well, it goes like this. A Lady walked in and went down the fishing section looking at some *fishing hooks.* I went up to her and very politely said, "Good morning, madam, you look like you could use some help." "Yes," she replied, "actually I do. My husband had a hernia operation, and he is out of action for a few weeks. We thought that it would be a good idea to go camping until he recovers and have a good rest."

"Excellent idea," I exclaimed and proceeded with the sale of the hooks. Then I sold her the line, a new fishing rod, outdoor chairs, and a BBQ. She then said, "I am spending more than I anticipated." I said, "You are making your husband happy." Then

I asked if they had a tent and she nodded yes. At this point I asked if she was afraid of spiders or other creatures, and she said, "Terrified! That's the reason I don't go camping often." I then asked if she likes camping, and she said, "I love it." I paused for a minute and then asked, "Why are you allowing the little creatures to deprive you from such pleasant experience? I have a solution for you. Imagine the wonderful times you can have with the whole family."

She frowned and said, "What do you mean?" I said, "With very little money I can sell you a caravan with all the facilities."

"Oh no," she said. "I have to call my husband." "Okay," I said, but before you do, let me show you a couple of them to have an idea." I then took her in the yard and showed her how beautiful the interior was with all the comforts, shower, cooker, the folding beds etc., etc. She was so excited that she called her husband and sold it to him. He said Okay under the condition that he chooses the colour. Very happy, she said, "I am coming to pick you up now," and so she did. She drove him in, and he stayed in the car because he couldn't walk. He picked the colour, and she signed up all the documents. As I was about to congratulate him, I looked at his car and said, "Oh no, your car is too small to tow this caravan." And that's how I sold him a new four-wheel drive, and my sale reached 89,000 dollars on my first day.'

Bappoo then said to the manager, '*Bernise stin vrisin, Je fernise abodon.*'

Moral
Be aware of smooth-talkers.

7. Bedassi ofkera na bari yiemada.
7. Πετάσσει όφκαιρα, να παρει γεμάτα.
7. Throws empty ones to get full ones.

Meaning
You give your empty glass to the barman as a hint to get a full one.

Used
Used when a 'sticky nose' hints to open a particular subject in order to optain information.

Example
Katina was one of the many gossipers in the village. She wanted to know if it was true that Dorothy had separated from her husband. When she ran into Dorothy's mum at the local shop, she kept on asking her questions related to Dorothy, trying to lead her into talking about her.

Bappoo then said, '*Bedassi ofkera, na bari yiemada.*'

Moral
Beware of inquisitive gossipers hinting.

8. Bodavristoo ospoo ftannis.
8. Ποταβρίστου ώσπου φτάννεις.
8. Stretch as far as you can reach.

Meaning
Take up only as much as you can handle.

Used
Used when one goes beyond one's means.

Example
Johnnie didn't want to take his father's advice to buy a cheaper car that he could afford and also become a more experienced driver on it. As soon as he got his licence he bought a very expensive car that he couldn't afford, and no money was left for the insurance. He drove an uninsured car, and now he doesn't have a car, because he had an accident that he was lucky to survive. The car was a write-off, and now not only has he lost the car but he is 30,000 dollars poorer as he is still liable for the payments on it.

That's when Bappoo says, '*Bodavristoo ospoo ftannis.*'

Moral
Do not exceed your limitations.

9. Boo loodoorga thkio eklishies, banda dis mias yiela dis.
9. Πού λουτουρκά δκιο εκκλησιές, πάντα της μιας γελά της.
9. Who preaches in two churches doesn't do justice to one.

Meaning
When you try to do two things in two different places at the same time, one of them misses out.

Used
Used when one tries to do two things in two places at the same time.

Example
Spiro has a little grocery store in the village and also owns a taxi. When he is driving the taxi he closes the shop, and of course he

loses customers when he is not there. It is clear that he couldn't do both jobs at the same time. That's when Bappoo says, *'Boo loodoorga thkio eklishies, banda dis mias yiela dis.'*

Moral
You can only be in one place at a time.

10. Boo jinia thkio laoos, hanni doos je doos thkio.
10. Πού τζυνιά δκιο λαούς, χάννει τους τζαι τους δκιο.
10. He who hunts two hares at the same time loses them both.

Meaning
If you try to shoot two running hares at the same time, you lose them both.

Used
Used when one attempts to do more than one quick action at the same time.

Example
A taxi driver at the airport spotted two tourists going to two different destinations. The greedy taxi driver tried to talk them both into getting in his cab. Before he knew it, they were gone with other taxis as they were not in a negotiating mood. Then he remembered Bappoos words: '*Boo jinia thkio laoos, hanni doos je doos thkio.*'

Moral
Concentrate on one target at a time.

11. Boo don sianon bodamon na foase.
11. Που τον σιανόν ποταμόν να φοάσαι.
11. Beware of the slow-flowing creek.

Apollo Bay, Victoria, Australia

Meaning
Slow-flowing creeks are usually quiet and unpredictable. Suddenly they flood and take everything in their path. You don't know when they will flood and are too risky to be trusted.

Used
Used when one usually is quiet and suddenly does something that was not expected of one.

Example
Petro's and Vasilis's Snow Trip on Mount Troodos

Petros and Vasilis are very good friends. They go everywhere together. Petros is a loud joker, and Vasilis is the quiet one.

One long weekend, they decided to go skiing up to Troodos Mountain in Cyprus. They were thirty minutes away from the top, and they stopped at a service station to refuel.

The attendant told them that they couldn't continue their drive up the mountain because the road was closed due to heavy snowfall.

Petros said, 'I am not going back to town. We'll drive to the nearest farmhouse and ask the farmer if he could accommodate us until the morning.' And so they did; they knocked at the door of the first farmhouse, and this most beautiful middle-aged lady opened the door. Vasilis's eyes popped out. Petros then said, 'We are so sorry to intrude, but we are stuck here and were wondering if you can let us stay here for the night.' She looked at them for a minute trying to sass them out. 'We'll pay you for it,' Petros said.

She then replied, 'Its okay, but you would have to sleep in the shed over there, because I am a widow and I don't want to start a gossip in the village.' They agreed and they couldn't thank her enough. She gave them a couple of blankets each and closed the door, and off they went to the shed.

The following morning they got up, thanked the lady, offered her some money, which she wouldn't accept, and they left.

Nine months later, Petros paid a visit to young, quiet Vasilis.

'Hi, Vasilis,' he said in a serious tone of voice. 'I want to ask you something, and I want the whole truth.'

Vasilis quite worried replied, 'Okay, what is it?'

Petros then asked, 'Do you remember nine months ago we went to Troodos skiing?'

'Yes, I do,' Vasilis answered.

'Do you remember we slept in that lady's shed?'

'Yes, I do,' he replied trembling.

'Now tell me, you little bastard, did you pay her a visit in her bedroom, in the middle of the night?'

Vasilis, feeling a bit embarrassed, said, 'Yes, actually I did, but no, she couldn't have been pregnant, impossible.'

Then Petros said, 'Did you give her my name and my address?'

Vasilis went yellow in the face. 'Yes, I did. I am sorry, Petros. I am so sorry. I shouldn't have done it.'

Petros then chased him around the house and when he caught up to him he put his head in a headlock and . . . gave him a big kiss on the forehead; then he said, 'It's okay, Vasilis. I am a very understanding friend.'

'Thanks, Petros, you are a real pal, but what brought that up?'

Petros showed him a letter and said, 'This is from her solicitor. She died and left me everything.'

Bappoo said, '*Boo don sian**o**n bodam**o**n na fo**a**se.*'

Moral
Beware of the quiet ones.

12. Boo isoon, boobode.
12. Που ήσουν, πούποτε.
12. Where were you? Nowhere.

Back to square one.

Meaning
All your efforts were wasted, and you were back to where you started . . .

Used
Used when one's efforts in doing something were wasted due to failure.

Example
Zavo's and Vasili's Partnership

Zavos had an idea to go into business with Vasili. They agreed to invest 10,000 pounds each to buy a truck, go to Ziyi to load it up with watermelons, and sell them around the villages. So they did. They went to Ziyi and bought 2,000 kg of watermelons worth 10,000 bakkires. They bought the watermelons at 5 bakkires per kg and sold them at 5 bakkires per kg. After a couple of days Vasilis said to Zavos, 'I think, Zavos, we are doing something wrong because I don't see any profits.' Zavos then reacted quite defensively and said, 'For God's sake, Vasili, give the business a chance. We have only just started.' Vasilis wasn't very happy, but after a week again he said, 'Hey, Zavos, I don't know what you think, but I think that something is seriously wrong because the money is getting less and less. We started with 10,000 bakkires, and now we only have 7,000. *Boo **is**oon, b**oo**bode.*'

Then Zavos scratched his head and said, 'I know what the problem is. The truck is too small. We will sell it and buy a larger one to fit more watermelons, and that's when we will make more money.'

Moral
Consider all aspects prior to committing.

13. Bolidehnidis ke erimospidis.
13. Πολυτεχνίτης τζαι ερημοσπίτης.
13. A Man of all trades lives in ruins.

Similar to English version: Jack of all trades, master of none.

Meaning
This refers to handymen who have basic skills in many trades but do not finish any.

Used
Used when one is a multi-tradesman but not fully qualified in anything and half finishes everything.

Example
Joe is a handyman who is a multi-tradesman and is not capable of finishing anything properly because he jumps from one project to another. Even if he finds a job, he is always underpaid because he is not fully qualified in anything.

Bappoo said, *'Bolidehnidis ke erimospidis.'*

Moral
Stick to what you know best.

14. Boo stillon, stillon anesin, osboo na vki i psishi doo.
14. Που στύλλον-στύλλον άνεσην, ώσπου να βκει η ψυσιή του.
14. From post to post grasping a breath, until death.

Meaning
One is dying and dragging himself along, resting from post to post, trying to take a breath.

Used
Used when things are not going very well and there are no signs of improvement whether in business or private life.

Example
A multinational chain of supermarkets has opened opposite a little corner grocery shop and has taken most of its customers, to the point where the little shop can't survive. Bappoo said, '*Boo stillon, stillon anesin osboo na vki i psishi doo.*'

Moral
If you can't correct it, divert.

D

1. Da bolla loyia eftoshia.
1. Τα πολλά λόγια εν φτώσια.
1. Too much talk brings poverty.

Meaning
Talking too much makes you poor.

Used
Used mainly by foremen to stop workers from talking and make them concentrate on their work.

Example
Vicki was working in a seafood-processing place, and she had a bad habit of talking too much. She was warned a few times that talking takes your concentration away from your work, but she didn't listen, until one day she was so busy talking that she packed the wrong fish in the wrong baskets. As a result of that they lost a customer and she lost her job.

Her husband then said to her, *'Da bolla loyia eftoshia.'*

Moral
Too much talk incurs losses.

2. Doo fronimoo do bethi, brin binasi mayirevi. 2. Του φρονίμου το παιδί πριν πεινάσει μαϊρέφκει.
2. Sensible people cook before they get hungry.

Angelo Karaiskakis's first visit to Australia with Mom and Dad, Koulli and Christalene, 2011

Meaning
Plan ahead, don't leave things to the last minute.

Used
Used to highlight the importance of planning ahead and not leaving things for the last minute.

Example
The Glory Box Story (True story)

I remember my mother had a large heavy box with a hinged lid that looked like a huge suitcase. I asked her what it was and she said that it was a glory box (*mbaoulo*). I then asked what she used it for, and she said, 'In here was my dowry.' It was a tradition that the mothers gave each one of their daughters a glory box with their dowry in it (known as *Brika*). It was all the essential household linen for the bedroom, dining room, etc. for when they got married. The mothers started collecting for the glory box from the time the girls started school. I asked why so early before they got married, and she said, '*Doo fronimoo do bethi, brin binasi mayirevi.*' Because those days most people were very poor, they didn't have money to buy what they needed, so they had to start early as they could afford them by accumulating little by little. A lot of them were hand-woven by the mother, aunties, or even friends in the village, and they all worked together as a team helping each other. Sometimes it took them months or years to finish a blanket. They had to be ready for when and if their fortune came knocking at their door and someone sent the proxy lady to ask for their hand in marriage.

Planning could make your life easier not only in business, but also in everyday family living.

The Chinese philosopher Confucius once said, 'If you don't plan before you leave home, the problem will come to your door.'

Management Test

How would you prioritise the following four tasks?

Like to do.
Urgent.
Important.
Need to do.

Put them in the correct order.

1. ⋯
2. ⋯
3. ⋯
4. ⋯

The correct answer is in following pages.

3. Do thendron bou lia, en ispazi.
3. Το δέντρον που λυά εν ισπάζει.
3. The tree that bends doesn't snap.

Meaning
The tree that is flexible is not likely to snap.

Used
It's used when dealing with a stubborn or opinionated person who never changes his/her mind.

Example
Constantinos was very upset because his son met a girl of a different religion and he wanted to marry her. Constantinos objected to that very strongly, to the point that he gave his son an ultimatum. 'You have to pick either her, or us,' he said.

Constantinos tried for several days to get his father to compromise, but it was impossible so he made a decision. He told his dad, 'Well, because it is about me and my life and not about you, Dad, and you don't respect my decision, you can play your power games by yourself. I pick the girl I love with or without you.'

He went ahead and got engaged, with the whole family attending but his father. After a year they were preparing for the wedding.

The whole family tried very hard to change his mind, but Constantino was adamant. His wife begged him to be flexible and compromise; otherwise it would break up the family. '*Do thendron boo lia, en ispazi,*' she said.

Eventually under the pressure of the whole family, he gave in and gave them his blessings for the wedding.

Moral
Flexibility prevents extremism.

4. Do eksibnon boollin, boo din moottin biannede.
4. Το έξυπνον πουλλίν που τη μούττην πιάνεται.
4. The smart bird gets caught by its beak.

Meaning
Smart people get in trouble because of overconfidence.

Used
Used when one gets in trouble due to overconfidence.

Example
Miss Theofilos's Overconfidence

The teacher asked the class if they had done their homework, and they all answered yes. He then called on Miss Theofilos to stand up.

'Can you tell me, Miss Theofilos, which part of the human body enlarges seven times its original size in the dark?'

She blushed and answered, 'How dare you ask me such a rude question and embarrass me! I come from a decent family, and I will report you to my parents and to the headmaster!'

The teacher, quite annoyed, asked her to sit down. Then he asked if anyone else wanted to answer the question. A few students raised their hands, and the teacher asked Johnnie to answer. Johnnie then stood up and said, 'The pupil of the eye, sir.'

'Correct,' said the teacher. 'As for you, Miss Theofilos, make sure tomorrow you come to school with your parents, and remember: 1. you haven't done your homework, 2. you have a dirty mind, and 3. one day when you get married, you will be a very disappointed wife. And don't forget, *Do eksibnon boollin, boo din moottin biannede.*'

Moral
Overconfidence can get you in trouble.

> *5. Do shinin doo horkadi monon en eftannen,*
> *je thiblon ftanni je berissevgi.*
>
> 5. Το σιηνίν του χωρκάτη μονόν εν έφταννεν
> τζαι διπλόν φτάννει τζαι Περισσεύκει.
>
> 5. The villager's rope is too short when it's single,
> but more than long enough when doubled.

Meaning

A villager took his donkey to the field to graze. He staked him in the middle of the field, away from the trees so he wouldn't reach to chew them up and destroy them. He was greedy and used the whole length of rope so the donkey could reach all the grass to graze, thus saving money feeding him at home.

The neighbour warned him that the rope was too long, but he said, 'Don't worry. It doesn't reach your trees.'

The next day he went to check on his donkey, and much to his amazement, all the trees around the donkey were chewed up and destroyed by it, including the neighbour's, and to top it off, he copped a ten-shilling fine from the ranger.

He then realised that being greedy and using the whole length of the rope was not a wise decision.

After this, he never used the rope single again. He was quite happy to use it double, which was shorter and stronger, to be on the safe side, even if it meant more work for him.

Used

It is used when one makes instantaneous and ill-thought decisions, takes short cuts to save time or money, and ends up paying more.

Example

Patrick decided to build his fence without a building permit to save the 200-dollar fee. He got caught, and the council made him demolish it and rebuild it, with an additional cost of 3,000 dollars. Bappoo then said, *'Do shinin doo horkadi monon en eftannen, je thiblon ftanni je berissevgi.'*

Moral

Ill-thought decisions could have unexpected and costly consequences.

6. *Do shillin soo je do bethin soo, obos da mathis.*
6. Το σιυλλί σου τζαι το παιδί σου όπως τα μάθεις.
6. It's how you train your puppy and your child.

Jim and Christalene, Johannesburg, S. Africa, 1975

Meaning
Your puppy's and your child's behaviour depends on their upbringing.

Used
Used when a child misbehaves.

Example
Children Grow Like Trees

My mother used to say that bringing up kids is like planting trees. You place a stake next to them, push it into the ground, and tie them on to it for support and protection from the wind and the rain until they grow up straight and strong.

After that, they can go in any direction they like, and you have no control.

Bappoo said, '*Do shillin soo je do bethin soo, obos da mathis.*'

Moral
Discipline begins from day one.

Koonia Bella (True story)

It was August 1976 in Boksburg, South Africa. My daughter Christalene was three years old and Angelo was one. We used to take them to the nearby park to play and put them on the swings. They sang 'Koonia, bella, koonia bella' as they swung. Little Angelo loved singing 'Bella, bella' going with the swing.

One night I went home after work, and my wife was putting him down to sleep in his cot, which was in our bedroom. We kissed him good night and left the room. A few hours later, I don't know how to say this, but we got sprang. As we were minding our own business, we heard him singing 'Bella bella'. We turned around and there he was standing up holding on the cot's side and was actually doing the movement of 'bella, bella' looking at us. We couldn't help bursting out laughing and told him to go back to bed because we were not doing 'koonia bella'.

If you think this was funny, wait and see what happened a few days later. His godparents, Freddy and Sofoulla, were coming for dinner that night with Sofoulla's mom, who was visiting them from Cyprus. Irene was serving little nibbles at that time and out of the blue Angelo came out of the bedroom with one of Christallenni's dolls. He placed it on the floor in front of all of us and lay on top of her singing 'Bella, bella'.

What happened then, I cannot describe. We all were in tears from laughter, and Freddy picked him up saying, 'That's my boy,' and gave him 20 rands.

7. Do min se melli min rodas.
7. Το μη σε μέλλει, μη ρωτάς.
7. Do not ask if it doesn't concern you.

Meaning
Don't get involved if it doesn't concern you.

Used
Used when one is inquisitive and asks a lot of questions.

Example
Katina is a very inquisitive person and pries in to other people's business. One day she met an acquaintance and asked him personal questions.

Her husband then said to her, '*Do min se melli min rodas.*'

Moral
Mind your own business.

8. *Do yinadin vkalli mmadin.*
8. Το γινάτι φκάλλει αμμάτι.
8. Stubbornness loses you an eye.

Meaning
A stubborn person can lose a lot more than what one bargains for.

Used
Used when one's stubbornness costs one a lot of money or effort. (Waste's time, money and effort to achieve something that is of no real benefit simply because he or she is stubborn.)

Example
Kiriakos's Scuba-Diving Experience

One day I went with my friend Kiriakos to Philip Island, Australia, to go scuba-diving and do some fishing with the spear gun. A couple of locals were sitting on the rocks watching us, and one of them said not to dive in, because this area was very dangerous. 'Sudden waves can throw you on to the rocks, and not many people come out alive.' I asked Kiriako to move further down and not to take any chances, but being a very stubborn man, he said no. 'Kyriako is here, there is no fear. I can handle any situation.' We had an argument earlier on because he was not supposed to dive by himself anyway. He knew that I didn't swim.

Ignoring everybody and everything, he jumped in, and I watched him disappear into the frothy waves. I was sitting on edge waiting for him to reappear. The locals were shaking their heads in disagreement, and I said, 'There is nothing I can do.'

After half an hour of fishing I said to him, 'Enough, let's go.' I could see the waves were getting higher and higher, and I was panicking and yelling at him to come out, but to no avail. Suddenly, the unthinkable happened, A huge, eight-metre wave came into the bay, and we all ran away only to see Kiriako flying up in the air and landing in a gap between rocks on a pile of seaweed.

We ran to his aid and got him out. One of the locals was a retired paramedic, and he checked him out. He was exhausted and trying to gasp a breath.

The paramedic said, 'You have no idea how lucky you are not to hit the rocks. I thought you wanted to commit suicide.'

I said to him, *'Do yinadin vkalli mmadin.'*

Moral
Stubbornness can harm your well-being and your wallet.

9. Dravame je as gleo.
9. Τράβα με τζ' ας κλαίω.
9. I refuse, but force me.

Similar to the expression: Twist my arm.

Meaning
Even if I refuse to accept something that I love, please insist.

Used
Used when an egoist wants to do something that he/she loves but wants it to be seen as if they are doing the others a favour.

Example
Mrs Portocallos was a member of a club, and she loved organising plays and theatres at various festivities for the club. She loved being the centre of attention, the cameras, the microphones, etc. She was so up herself that she was too proud to ask the

committee to let her do a play for a forthcoming event. She secretly would ask others to tell the committee that there was a big demand for her plays, so the committee would approach her first. She wanted it to look like she was doing them a favour.

When it eventually happened, her reaction would be 'Well, I am busy, but since you want me to do it so badly I will do it for you.'

That's when Bappoo says, *'Dravame j'as gleo.'*

Moral
Don't play hard to get.

E

1. *En'mitsis amman rotsis.*
1. Εν μιτσής αμμάν ροτσίς.
1. He is little, but rocky.

Meaning
That one is small but tough like a rock.

Used
Used as a compliment when one is little but tough, capable, and valuable.

Example
Freddy was only just 1.4 metres tall. He applied for a job at the local cooperative of carob growers. The foreman looked at him said that it would require a lot of lifting and carrying of 20-kg bags.

Freddy said, 'I have no problem with that.'

The foreman reluctantly gave him a chance to try him for a couple of days. Much to his surprise, Freddy was stronger and faster than everyone else despite his size.

When the manager saw him, he asked the foreman why he'd hired that little man. He then replied, *'En mitsis amman rotsis.'*

Moral
Don't underestimate small people.

> *2. Epien o ftohos na armasti, je'mitchanen ei nihta.*
> 2. Επήεν ο φτωχός ν' αρμαστεί τζ' εμίτσιανεν η νύχτα.
> 2. The poor went to get married, and the night shrank.

Meaning
It seems like whatever a poor person tries to do, something always goes wrong.

Used
Used when a poor person decides to do something and whatever can go wrong, goes wrong.

Example
Zavos took his watermelons to the market to sell and make some money to pay his bills, and he was stunned to see that nobody was interested in buying them.

He was getting a bit worried, and when he asked why, he was told that last week some other farmers had been selling watermelons with a high content of hormones in them, and a few people died from it.

The poor man had no idea what hormones were, but he copped it. He then said, *'Epien o ftohos na armasti, je mitchanen i nihta.'*

Moral
Don't leave anything to chance.

3. Evalan mas da thkio mas bothkia s'enan babootsin.
3. Εβάλαν μας τα δκιο μας πόδκια σ' ένα παπούτσι.
3. They put both of our feet in one shoe.

They made us tighten our belts.

Meaning
We were forced into an awkward situation.

Used
Used when one is put in a position to lower one's standards.

Example
The Greek government introduced austerity measures in order to get out of the financial crisis. They cut wages, reduced the standard of living, and made the Greek people 'put both feet in one shoe'. *Evalan mas da thkio mas bothkia s'enan babootsin.*

Moral
When you have financial problems, lower your standards.

4. Evcalen onoman o theristis jeppesen je jimadoon.
4. Εφκαλεν όνομαν ο θεριστής τζ' έππεσεν τζαι τζοιμάτουν.
4. The reaper made a name for himself and couldn't care less.

Meaning
Because a reaper was known to be the best, he was taking it easy.

Used
Used when one becomes a celebrity and doesn't care after.

Example
Years ago before all the agricultural machinery was invented, farmers used to gather the whole family and friends to harvest their cereal crops. They shared the burden, helping each other so they didn't have to pay wages, particularly in small villages where farms were small and they all knew each other. The work was done by the reapers using a hand-held tool called a sickle (*threbani*). This was like a curved knife with a handle, and it

had a radius of approximately 35–40 cm. The reapers would sing and joke, trying to keep their morale high during the hot summer days of harvesting. They put a lot of pride in to their work, and they would compete against each other to see who was the fastest in the village. It was an honour to carry the title of the best reaper. Sometimes it would go to their head. As a result of that they would take it easy and wouldn't care less, to the point that they would fall asleep. That's when Bappoo says, '**E**vcalen **o**noman o therist**is** j**e**ppesen je jim**a**doon.'

Moral
Humbleness brings respect.

5. Evcalen i glossa moo mallia.
5. Εφκαλεν η γλώσσα μου μαλιά.
5. I grew hair on my tongue.

Meaning

This means that when you say something repeatedly, you grow hair on top of your tongue. It is a metaphor for 'I warned you so many times.'

Used

Used when your repeated warnings fall on deaf ears.

Example

I warned my son not to park his car on the nature strip because he would get booked one day. Of course he wouldn't take any notice until one day he did get booked and copped a 90-dollar fine. That's when Bappoo says, '*Evcalen i glossa moo mallia,* from telling you that.'

Moral

You can only bring something to one's attention once.

6. *Evkiges sdon horon, brebi na horepsis.*
6. Εφκήκες στο χορόν πρέπει να χορέψεις.
6. You get on the dance floor, you must dance.

Pegasus Dance Academy at Federation Square, Melbourne, 2009

Meaning
When you find yourself on the dance floor, you have to dance to any tune.

Used
Used when you find yourself in a situation where you have to act unwillingly.

Example
The motor of my delivery truck had blown up one day, and I took it to a 'reputable' motor reconditioned in Melbourne for a changeover. I got quoted $3,500 all up. The next day I had a phone call from them saying that the gears are worn out and it

would cost an extra $1,200. Then they called again to say the belts need to be changed, an extra $300. Then again they called, with the hoses and water pump needed to be changed, another $ 800. Then the alternator etc. etc ... By the time I realised their extortionist methods, I couldn't back out. I was already 'on the dance floor'.

Bappoo said, *'Evkiges sdon horon, brebi na horepsis'"*

Moral
If you start something, you have to finish it.

7. Elimbisen i rka sta sica, je enna fa je da sicofilla.
7. Ελίμπησεν η ρκα στα σύκα τζ' εννά φα τζαι τα συκόφυλλα.
7. The old lady loved figs so much that
she would even eat the leaves.

Similar to the English version:
I gave you my finger, and you took my hand.

Meaning
When you are too generous, some can take advantage of you.

Used
Used when you give something and one keeps coming back demanding more, taking advantage of you.

Example
I ordered a cubic metre of sand to finish my cobblestones in my driveway. My neighbour asked if he could borrow a bucketful of sand to add to his son's sandpit. I said that was okay. But then he kept on coming back, taking bucketfuls.

I then said to him, '*Elimbisen i rka sta sika, j enna fa je da sikofilla.*'

Moral
Don't allow others to take advantage of you.

8. Enan shelionin en ferni din anniksin.
8. Ένα σιελιόνιν εν φέρνει την άννοιξη.
8. One swallow doesn't bring spring.

Meaning
It is well known that spring brings a lot of migrating birds such as swallows, which look for a warmer climate. When the locals see the swallows, they know it is spring. It doesn't mean though that if you see one swallow in winter that spring is coming.

Used
Used when one rushes to make a major decision with only one evidence.

Example
I was playing golf for the very first time, and on the ninth hole I scored a birdie. I was so excited that I told my teammate I wanted to play golf with Tiger Woods. He burst out laughing and said, **'*Enan shelionin en ferni din anniksin.*'**

Moral
Get all the facts prior to jumping to conclusions.

*9. Ennen da rasa boo camnoon don baban,
en o babas boo camni da rasa.*
9. Εννεν τα ράσα που κάμνουν τον παπάν,
εν ο παπάς που κάμνει τα ράσα.
9. It is not the gown that makes a priest, but
the priest that makes the gown.

Meaning
Wearing a gown doesn't make you a priest.

Used
Used when one attempts to be someone that one is not.

Example
Johnnie put on his brother's police cap and said, 'Look, Dad, I am a policeman!' Dad then laughed and said, 'A uniform doesn't make you a policeman.' Bappoo then said, *'Ennen da rasa boo camnoon don baban, en o babas boo camni da rasa.'*

Moral
Don't be deceived by appearance.

10. Eminamen san eminen, o Hajimarcos bersi,
elipsandoo da garvoona jenishen na thoolepsi.
10. Εμείναμεν σαν έμεινεν ο Χατζημάρκος πέρσυ,
ελείψαν του τα κάρβουνα τζ' ένεισιεν να δουλέψει.
10. We got stuck like Hajimarcos did last
year, when he ran out of coal.

Meaning

We are in trouble now like Hajimarcos was last year, when he ran out of charcoals and couldn't work as a blacksmith.

Used

Used when one's activity or festivity is interrupted due to unforseen problems.

Example
Spiro went for a Sunday drive out in the countryside with his wife. As they were approaching Woodend, the car sounded like it was missing a couple of times, and then it stopped.

Spiro then frowned and yelled, 'Oh no! I forgot to put petrol in the car!'

His wife then said, *'Eminamen san eminen, o Hajimarcos bersi, elipsandoo da garvoona jenishen na thoolepsi.'*

Moral
Do not leave anything to chance.

***11.** Enme da hronia boo gadevenni o noos.*
11. Εν με τα χρόνια που κατεβαίνει ο νους.
11. Maturity comes in time.

Meaning
Children naturally do silly things until they mature in time.

Used
Used when we see hyperactive children acting silly.

Example
(True story)

One day I came home from work, and I heard my son yelling, 'Help, help!'

I rushed in and saw him in the passage hanging upside down from the top of the wall. The passage was quite narrow, and he could reach from one wall to the other, shoulder-feet. He used to walk up and down the one wall, with his back on the opposite wall. That day the pressure against the wall pushed his heels through the plaster, and of course he ended up hanging upside down with his feet hooked in the plaster.

I took him to the doctor to check him up, and I asked the doctor. If he was mentally okay, because he was hyperactive and doing silly things.

The doctor smiled and said, 'There is definitely something wrong, but he will be okay when he grows up.'

I said, 'What is the problem, Doctor?'

He said, '*He is a kid*!' And he advised us to cut down on food and drinks that have high content of sugar and preservatives.

Then I remembered Bappo's words, '*Enme da hronia boo gadevenni o noos.*'

Moral
Let the kids be kids but guide them.

12. En mathimena da voona boo da shionia.
12. Εν μαθημένα τα βουνά που τα σιόνια.
2. The mountains are used to the snow.

Jim on a business trip. Loucano, Switzerland, 1987

Meaning
People become accustomed to conditions when they live in harsh conditions.

Used
Used when one works in extreme conditions and you express concern.

Example
Miners working in the hot sand of the desert usually sweat and are covered in dust. You express your sympathy for them, and they respond with a smile, 'Don't worry, the mountains are used to the snow.' Bappoo said, **'*En mathimena da voona boo da shionia.*'**

Moral
People become accustomed to any conditions.

> *13. Egamenda shionin je yastrin.*
> 13. Εκαμεν τα σιόνιν τζαι γαστρίν.
> 13. Stuffed everything up.

Meaning
One failed to achieve what one was bragging about.

Used
Used to mock the one that failed to deliver and proved to be only 'talk and no action'.

Example
The new manager was criticising the former manager and promised to save the company from bankruptcy but it looks like *'Egamenda shionin je yastrin'* because they are in receivership.

Moral
Don't take up a task that's not within your qualifications.

14. Ebian je d'avga je do galathin.
14. Επήαν τζαι τ' αυκά τζαι το καλάθι.
14. You lost both, the eggs and the basket.

Lost: Lock, stock, and barrel.

Meaning You lost everything.

Used
Used when one loses everything.

Example
There was a farmer selling eggs. Someone approached him and said, 'I want to buy the whole basket of them.' The farmer agreed to give him the basket to take home and to bring back the empty one with the money, but he never returned, so he lost everything, the eggs and the basket. Then Bappoo said, '*Ebian je d'avga je do galathin.*'

Moral
Be careful who or what you put your trust in.

15. Ebien yia mallin je irten gooremenos.
15. Επήε για μαλλίν τζαι ήρτεν κουρεμένος.
15. He went for hair and returned with his hair cut.

The Ioannou brothers 2008 reunion. Left to right: Kiriakos, Stelios, Thimitrakis (Jim), and Efthimios (John)

Meaning
One got the opposite results to what one expected.

Used
Used when you are quite confident you could achieve something but unexpectedly you have the opposite outcome.

Example
He went to the police to complain about a car accident, and they charged him for negligence. *Ebien yia mallin je irten gooremenos.*

Moral
Do your homework and don't underestimate the enemy.

*16. Eth**o** kara**v**ia hannonde, je i jir**a** hten**i**zede.*
16. Εδώ καράβκια χάννουνται τζαι η τζυρά χτενίζεται.
16. The ship is sinking, and the madam is brushing her hair.

Meaning

The ship was sinking, the captain was calling everyone to abandon the ship, and Madam Sousou was more concerned about her looks and hair.

Used

Used when one selfishly pays more attention to one's own trivial things, ignoring a disaster happening around one.

Example

The ship was sinking, the captain was calling everyone to abandon ship, and Madam Sousou was more concerned about her looks and hair. That's when Bappoo says, '*Eth**o** kara**v**ia hannonde, je i jir**a** hten**i**zede.*'

Moral

Consider others.

17. Efaamen don voon, Je eminen mas o nooros.
17. Εφάαμεν τον βουν τζ' έμεινεν μας ο νούρος.
17. We ate the whole ox but the tail.

Meaning
We have almost finished a project except for one minor thing.

Used
Used as an encouragement to others to continue working on a long project that is almost completed.

Example
We were picking olives one day out in the field with all my brothers and grandparents. After a long day's work it was time to go home, and my father said, 'We have one tree left, so let's finish it so we don't have to come back here tomorrow.'

We all started complaining and he said, 'Come on, *efaamen don voon, Je eminen mas o nooros.*'

Moral
Persistence brings achievement.

18. Egamen don psillon gamilon.
18. Εκαμεν το ψύλλον κάμηλον.
18. He made a camel out of a nit.

Meaning

One exaggerated, to the point that made a tiny bug as large as a camel.

Used

Used when people exaggerate and make things much bigger or better than what they really are.

Example

Vasili was telling everybody about the huge 50 kg pumpkin that he produced and showing them photos, bragging about it. The mayor of the village, not to be outdone, said, 'This is nothing. You should see the 3 m cucumber I produced last year.'

Knowing him how he exaggerates, everybody laughed and Bappoo said, *'Egamen don psillon gamilon.'*

Moral

Don't believe everything you hear.

19. En o yaros doo Hodjia, boo don emathhen na men droi.
19. Εν ο γάρος του Χότζια που τον έμαθεν να μεν τρώει.
19. Hodjia taught his donkey not to eat.

Meaning
Hodjia used false economy. He tried to save money by not feeding the donkey, and it cost him dearly.

Used
Used when one makes thoughtless decisions in order to save money without considering all aspects and, as a result, one suffers heavy loses.

Example
Hodjia was paying too much money to feed his donkey. He came up with the idea of teaching him not to eat in order to save money. He figured out that he could save two shillings a day by not feeding him. For twenty days he didn't feed the donkey, and Hojia was thrilled that he had saved forty shillings already. The twenty-first day he found the donkey dead on the floor. He was

devastated and said; 'I can't believe my luck! Now that I have trained him not to eat, he died on me, the bugger!'

Moral

Instantaneous and ill-thought decisions can have unexpected and costly consequences.

20. Evalan don aloobon na ylebi des ornithes.
20. Εβάλαν τον αλουπόν να βλέπει τες όρνιθες.
20. They put a fox to guard the henhouse.

Meaning
They trusted a fox that loves eating chickens to guard the hen house.

Used
Used when an untrustworthy person is entrusted valuables or is given a responsible position.

Example
Peter was an alcoholic, and he was recently employed as a storeman in a bottle shop (selling alcoholic drinks). After a few days, he started acting funny, until they realised that he was consuming lots of alcohol. The manager was informed about what happened and also that he was actually an alcoholic. Bappoo then said, '*Evalamen don aloobon na ylebi des ornithes.*'

Moral
Beware of people with bad reputation.

21. Evalen don nooron doo mes d'ashielia doo.
21. Εβαλεν τον νούρον του μεσ' τα σιέλια του.
21. He put his tail between his legs.

Meaning
Behaving just like a dog that puts his tail between his legs when you catch him doing something wrong.

Used
Used when you expose someone for a wrongdoing, and embarrassed, he/she cannot look you in the eye.

Example
Vasili hid when he went to the club because he couldn't face Petros. He had unjustly gossiped against Petros, who heard about it, and now Vasili, embarrassed, went and apologised, *'Evalen don nooron doo mes d'ashielia doo.'*

Moral
If you are at fault, keep your face up and apologise.

22. Eyio straonno je boolo je soo amblebe je yoraze.
22. Εγιώ στραώννω τζαι πουλώ τζ' εσού άμπλεψε τζαι γόραζε.
22. I blind you and sell, and you look and buy.

Meaning
The salesmen usually tell you what you want to hear in order to make a sale, and it would be wise to check if what they say is true.

Used
Used when you buy something and it's not what you were told it was.

Example
Hodjia bought another donkey after the other one died. He paid the money and took him home. He was told that he was only three years old, but when they checked his teeth (that is how they check their age), they discovered that he was actually nine years old and was not worth the money that he paid. Bappoo then said, '*Eyio straonno je boolo je soo amblebe je yoraze.*'

Moral
Always double-check before you pay anything you buy.

The Canary That Wouldn't Sing (Joke)

Giuseppe, a young Italian from Cecily was getting ready to board a cruise ship from Piraeus, Greece. Babbi, an older man approached him, carrying a small cage with a yellow canary in it. He lifted it up to show Giuseppe the canary and said, 'Look, senior, it's the last one, and I want to go home. Normally I sell for 3,000 drachmas, but if you give me 2,000, you can have it, so I can go home.' Giuseppe loved canaries and said, 'I'll give you

1,000 for it.' Babbi reluctantly accepted, but Giuseppe was also a bit hesitant. 'I am sorry, signor, but I don't have any more Greek money on me. Would you accept a cheque?' Babbi did accept the cheque and handed the cage with the yellow canary to the Italian as he was climbing up the stairs of the ship. As the ship started to move and everyone was waving goodbye, Giuseppe yelled, 'Hey, seignior, if you think you'll be able to cash that cheque, you have another thing coming, ha.'

Babbi then said, 'Oh yeah? If you think that the painted sparrow I gave you would ever sing, you have another thing coming, ha-ha-ha.'

*23. En **o**ksina da stafília, el**a**len i aloob**oo** boo en d**a**ftannen.*
23. Εν οξυνα τα σταφυλια, ελαλεν ι
αλουπου που εν τα εφταννεν.
23. The fox couldn't reach the grapes
and said that they were sour.

Meaning
The fox couldn't reach the grapes. She was too proud to admit it and gave the excuse that they were sour.

Used
Used when one doesn't want to show weakness by admitting failure and gives poor excuses.

Example
Aesop's Fable

A hungry fox saw some fine bunches of grapes hanging from a vine that was trained along a high trellis and did his best to reach them by jumping as high as he could into the air. But it was all in vain for they were just out of reach, so he gave up trying and walked away with an air of dignity and unconcern, remarking, 'I thought those grapes were ripe, but I see now they are quite sour.'

Andrew took his girlfriend out one night, and they were looking at all the beautiful, mouth-watering cakes through the window of a confectionery shop. Andrew loved baklava, and he could hardly resist, but he had no money left. He said to his girlfriend, 'I think we'll give them a miss because they don't look very fresh.' Smart girl as she was, she said smiling, 'Doesn't matter, darling, if they are not very fresh, my shout.'

That's when Bappoo says, '*En **o**ksina da stafilia, elalen i aloob**oo** boo en d**a**ftannen.*'

Moral
Poor excuses can give away your incompetence.

24. *Ela bappoo, na soo thikso da ambelia soo.*
24. Έλα παππού να σου δείξω τ' αμπέλια σου.
24. Grandpa, let me show you your vineyards.

Meaning
A young person tells an old and experienced person how and what to do.

Used
Used when a young person undermines the seniority, experience, and wisdom of older people and disrespectfully tells them how things should be done.

Example
The Smart Apprentice (True story)

One of my apprentices got his certificate after completing a four-year training course while still working. The following day, I noticed a change in his attitude. When I asked him what the problem was, he replied quite arrogantly, 'You can't tell me what to do now as I am a fully qualified tradesman like you (implying that now he knows everything).'

I smiled and said to him, 'I like you. You remind me of me when I was your age. That shows you have passion for what you do, but remember one thing, my dear boy. That certificate you just got is only one of the ten tools that you need for the job, the other nine 'tools' are called *experience* and you get one every ten years, which means that you keep learning until you die.

'You can use your initiative and try new methods of which we all can learn as well, but remember, there is always someone ahead of you with more 'tools' than you, and you have to respect that. Nobody gets to know everything because every day something new appears that the new tradespeople don't know.'

Bappoo said, **'Ela bappoo, na soo thikso da ambelia soo.'**

Moral
Experience and wisdom cannot be bought or made over a night. It comes with time.

25. *Egi*li*sen do stoo*ppoman je *i*vren do la*ve*zin.
24. Ετζύλησεν το στούππωμα τζαι ήβρεν το λαβέζι.
24. The lid found its pot.

Meaning
Perfect, much like the pot and the lid.

Used
Used mainly in partnerships when the pair is compatible with each other.

Example
The Tomato Fight (True story)

When my wife and I first came to Australia, we lived with my in-laws for a few months until we bought our own house. One night they went visiting, and we were in a funny silly mood. We were mocking around doing crazy things, throwing peanuts at each other, which eventually developed into full-scale tomato fight in the kitchen; the walls were covered with smashed tomatoes with the juice running down, and everything was in a mess. We were laughing so much we couldn't stand on our feet.

The funniest thing was when the door opened suddenly and my in-laws were there. They returned unexpectedly and saw the mess and us covered in smashed tomatoes. We looked at the expression on their faces and burst out laughing. We were in hysterics. My father-in-law then said, *'Egilisen do stooppoman je ivren do lavezin.'* The worst thing was the spring cleaning of the house.

Moral
Compatibility is very important in a marriage or relationship.

***26.** Etsi kkelle, etsi kshioorafin theli.*
26. Ετσι κκελλέ, έτσι ξιουράφι θέλει.
26. Such a head deserves such a shaver.

English version: You were asking for it, or don't play with fire.

Meaning
Whatever happens to you taking dangerous risks you were asking for it.

Used
Used when one harms oneself taking unnecessary risks.

Example
When youngsters risk their lives seeking thrill, they do stupid and dangerous things such as train surfing, hit a bridge, and get badly hurt.

Bappoo then says, **'*E*tsi kkell*e*, *e*tsi kshioor*a*fin th*e*li.'**

Moral
You can harm yourself acting dangerously, and it can be seen as stupidity for taking such risks.

F

1. Fain na famen eneshi, Je theloomen rebanakia yia oreksin.
1. Φαΐν να φάμεν εν έσιει τζαι θέλουμεν ρεπανάκια για όρεξη.
1. If you don't have food, you don't look for appetisers.

Meaning
It is pointless to look for appetisers if you don't have food to eat.

Used
Used when one looks for luxuries at a time that one cannot even afford the essentials.

Example
A newly married couple moved recently into a new house. They just managed to gather sufficient money to pay for the deposit on the house. They needed furniture and curtains and other essentials, but they didn't have money. Next day they were discussing purchasing a 5,000-dollar chandelier because it would look good in the entrance. Bappoo then said, *'Fain na famen eneshi, Je theloomen rebanakia yia oreksin.'*

Moral
Don't go beyond your means.

2. Fteon doo da rooha doo.
2. Φταίουν του τα ρούχα του.
2. He is so agitated, he blames his clothes.

Meaning

One is so pissed off that takes one's anger out on anything and everything, even on one's clothes.

Used

Used when one is agitated and gets mad at anything and everything.

Example

A boy broke up with his girlfriend and was so upset and angry that no one could talk to him. His mother then said, '*Fteon doo da rooha doo.*'

Moral

When you are calm, your decisions are more accurate.

3. Fakkoon doo baba meh da brosfora.
3. Φακκούν του παπά με τα πρόσφορα.
3. They hit the priest with the votive bread.

St Marina's Church, Ora Village, 1983

Meaning
In the Greek Orthodox religion, parishioners take whole loaves of bread to church in order for the priest to pray for their dead in a memorial service, or to celebrate a name day as a votive.

The bread is called *prosforo* (from the Greek verb *prosfero*), which means 'give as a gift'. The priest, after the service, cuts some in small cubes, gives some to the congregation, and the rest he takes home to feed his family.

Used
Used when a proud person is given something beneficial and gives the impression that he or she is only accepting it because they were put in a spot.

Example

Margaret works in a restaurant as a dishwasher, and every now and then the boss gives her leftover meat, vegies, etc. She always says, 'Don't worry, I am okay. I don't need them.' But she always takes them.

The chef then says to her, *'Fakk**oo**n doo bab**a** me da br**o**sfora.'*

Moral

Take what you deserve.

4. *Filae da rooha soo, nahis da misa.*
4. Φύλαε τα ρούχα σου νάσιεις τα μισά.
4. Safeguard your clothes to have only half of them.

Meaning
Even if you do safeguard your possessions, you still can lose half, so imagine if you didn't.

Used
It's used to emphasise the importance of protecting one's loved ones, property, and possessions.

Example
Why I Am Not Allowed to Catch the Train, Daddy? (True story)

The following conversation took place between my daughter and me when she was fifteen years old.

It was a winter Saturday night after dinner, when she came to me and hesitantly asked me if she could catch the train to the city with other girls.

I turned around and without any hesitation answered, 'Absolutely not,' in a non-negotiable tone. She then replied, 'Why, Daddy? You allowed Angelo one day, why not me just because I am a girl?'

I said, 'Yes, darling, exactly right.'

'What's the difference?' she asked.

I smiled at her and said, 'Well, if you don't know the difference between a boy and a girl, it's an additional reason why I shouldn't let you.'

She then said, 'I know the difference, but why is he allowed and I am not'?

I then went and sat next to her, put my arm around her shoulders, and said, 'The girls, darling, have something that the boys are after, particularly those boys that are idiots, and there are quite a few of them out there. This exposes the girls to a much, much greater danger than the boys.'

She then replied, 'The boys have something that the girls are after, too, Daddy.'

'Ah ha,' I said. 'But there is a little detail that you don't know, darling. Those boys only need a shower, have a wash, and end of the story. The girls on the other hand, in nine months' time can end up with a belly up to their nose, and this can scar them for life.'

She then replied, 'I know, Dad, but I know what to do. Don't you trust me?'

I said, 'Yes, I do, darling, but it's not a matter of trust. It's a matter of safety. You are only fifteen. I trust you to go in the forest, but I don't trust the tigers and I love you too much to risk it.'

She looked at me and, after a short pause, replied: 'Okay, Dad. I understand.'

It is disappointing to live in a society where we have to deprive our kids of their freedom to explore, but sometimes we have to face the reality and 'be cruel to be kind'. If they are too young to understand, it's the parents' obligation to keep them safe until they are old enough to understand and be in a better position to protect themselves, regardless whether they are boys or girls.

Some might think that I am been overprotective, but there would be no chance I would have compromised the safety of my little girl.

Moral
Prevention is better than cure.

G

1. Gootsi stravi ston Ain Bandeleimonan.
1. Κουτσοί, στραβοί στον Αην Παντελεήμονα.
1. Lame and blind to Saint Pandeleimon.

Meaning
Saint Panteleimon made a name that cures people with disabilities and everyone went to him to be cured.

Used
Used when one is often taken advantage of because is kind-hearted and giving and attracts many people that are in need.

Example
Odysseas was a kind handyman. He helped a friend to repair his leaking roof at no charge.

Then another acquaintance heard about it and asked Odysseas if he could help him fix his toilet at no charge. Then another, then another, and before he knew it, he had no time for himself. That's when Bappoo said, *'Gootsi stravi ston Ain Banteleimonan.'*

Moral
Don't go over the limit.

2. Galeston is don yamon soo, na soo bi je'abo hronoo.
2. Κάλεστον στον γάμο σου να σου πει τζαι του χρόνου.
2. Invite one to your wedding to wish you
to get married again next year.

Meaning
Metaphorically it means that when you deal with idiots you can expect idiotic comments.

Used
Used when you trust an idiot, and with the first chance he/she betrays you.

Example
Nick met a refugee that came to Australia. He gave him a job and helped him get on his feet. He was very appreciative up until he settled in his own apartment. One day they had an argument because every time Nick asked him for a favour he refused, giving excuses.

Bappoo then said, *'Galeston is don yamon soo, na soo bi je abo hronoo.'*

Moral
Be careful who you deal with.

3. Galion arya bara bode.
3. Κάλιον αργά παρά ποτέ.
3. Better late than never.

Meaning
It's better if you do something late than not do it at all.

Used
Used as an encouragement to one to start something that one believes is too late for it.

Example
Magdalena was an eighteen-year-old orphan, who was committed to raise her two little brothers after she lost her parents in a car accident. She always wanted to study law, but her commitment to raise the kids didn't allow her to do so. When she was thirty-five, she gave up the idea as she thought it was too late for studies. Her friends encouraged her that it was never too late, and she decided to do it. Now at the age of forty-two she is a proud holder of a law degree. Bappoo then said, *'Galion arya bara bode.'*

Moral
Never give up. It is never too late.

*4. **Ga**lion yaoor**o** thinne bara yaooro yirevke.*
4. Κάλιον γαουρόδιννε παρά γαουρογύρευκε.
4. Better tie the donkey now than look for him later.

Meaning
It's better to tie your donkey now to be sure it doesn't run away, than looking for it later.

Used
Used when one doesn't take preventative measures and leaves things to chance.

Example
The Adventure of Vasili

Vasili was a vegetable farmer producing cucumbers, tomatoes, zucchinis, etc. He used to load his donkey with all his goods and take them to the market in Larnaca. One day he lost his donkey, because in the morning rush he forgot to tie him down. No matter how hard he tried, he couldn't find him. It was getting dark, and he didn't know what to do. He missed the last bus to the village, so he decided to go to the nearest hotel to spend the night. He went up to the girl at the reception desk, exhausted from running around all day, and asked for a room. She looked at him and said, 'I am really sorry, Bapoo (grandpa), but we are fully booked.'

He then looked around and said, 'I am very tired, dear. I don't mind spending the night even on a couch, if it's okay.'

The young lady felt so sorry for him that she told him to follow her upstairs and took him to a room with a double bed. She said,

'Bappoo, this is the room of a young, newly married couple. If you promise me to keep quiet, I will let you sleep under the bed for the night, just to help you out.'

Vasili promised that he would, thanked her, and rolled under the bed on a blanket.

As he was about to fall asleep, the young couple walked in. They had a drink, a few kisses, got undressed, and went to bed. Of course, being newly married, they were not expected to go to sleep in a hurry.

As he was telling her how beautiful she was, he looked into her eyes and said, 'Darling, in your beautiful eyes I can see the whole world'.

On hearing this, the old man yelled out, 'Do you see my donkey anywhere?'

Poor Vasili got kicked out and ended up in the streets until the next morning. So he learnt that *Galion yaooro thinne bara yaooro yirevke.*

Moral
Prevention is better than cure.

5. Galion enan je sto sherin, bara theka je carterin.
5. Κάλιον ένα τζαι στο σιέριν παρά δέκα τζαι καρτέρει.
5. Better one in hand than ten later.

English equivalent: Better the egg now than the chicken later.

Meaning
Better to have one in your hands now than ten later.

Used
Used when one take's chances and gambles in order to gain more.

Example
George was offered $1,800,000 for a block of land that he had bought for $400,000. Despite his wife's advice to sell it, he said, 'No, if I wait a couple of years to subdivide it, it would be worth double.' His wife then said, *'Galion enan je sto sherin, bara theka je carterin.'*

A year later they received a letter from the state government notifying them that the land would be acquired for the new freeway and offered them $1,100,000 as valued by the government.

Moral
Take what is guaranteed.

6. *Gallittera na soo vki do mmadin, bara donoman.*
6. Καλλίττερα να σου φκεί το μάτι παρά το όνομα.
6. Better to lose an eye than your name.

Meaning
It is better to lose an eye than to lose your reputation.

Used
It's used when one's reputation is damaged, or as an advice to prevent that from happening.

Example
Harry's Koupes

Harry used to make *koupes* (a traditional Cypriot food, mincemeat and herbs in crushed wheat pockets). He made such a good name for himself and his *koupes* that people came from all over the town to buy them. His opposition was not doing very well, and being a person of bad reputation and no ethics, he did something really bad.

He killed a cat and put its fur in Harry's rubbish bin, in the aisle, with half of it hanging outside the bin. Of course, it didn't take long for the word to spread in town that Harry was using cat meat in his *koupes*. That was enough to destroy his reputation and, in turn, his business. You can see now why Bappoo said, '*Gallittera na soo vki do mmadin, bara do onoman.*'

Moral
Having a good reputation pays.

Maria's Reputation (Joke)

Young Maria went to her grandma and told her that she had met a boy and she was going out with him for the first time on Saturday.

Grandma then said to her, 'Listena herea, Maria, and listena gooda! You have a to be very, very carefula because the boys are aftera one thinga only. You must say no, no, no, grandma said I am a decent girl. Especially don't let any of them lie on top of you, whatever you do, because if you do, you will fall pregnant and you will disgrace our whole family.'

The following day Maria went up to grandma, very excited, and said to her, 'Grandma! Grandma, you were right. He wanted to do exactly what you told me, and he wanted to lie on top of me too, just like you said!'

'Oh my God!' Grandma replied in shock. 'I hope you didn't let him and disgrace our family.'

Maria then said, 'What do you think, Grandma? I am not that stupid to disgrace my family. I lay on top of him to disgrace his family!'

7. Galos – galos o shiros mas, evkigen halaziaris.
7. Καλός-καλός ο σιοίρος μας έφκηκεν χαλαζιάρης.
7. Our best pig turned out to have a disease.

Meaning
We were bragging about having the best pig, and it turned out to be inferior.

Used
Used when we value and praise something or someone, and much to our disappointment, they turn out to be inferior.

Example
The Flimsy Boat (True story)

The daughter of a friend named Vicki, who is in her late twenties, met a boy by the name Alexis. After going out with him for a few months, they were both satisfied that they were made for each other and could spend the rest of their life together. She brought him home and introduced him to the family. Alexis was accepted with open arms because he was always doing the right thing. Everyone loved him and thought he was the best thing since sliced bread. They both worked and both went through unemployment period and back to work again. They went through thick and thin together, and three years down the track, they decided to get engaged to make it more official.

It was then that the problem started. Alexis started getting cold feet. It was then that the responsibilities as a husband and perhaps as a father later hit him and scared the hell out of him. He wanted out.

He wanted out any which way he could, and he started pulling all Vicki's faults out of a hat, one by one. He blamed her for many things. She loved him so much that she was prepared to do anything to change for him. She was devastated, and the parents were devastated as well.

That week I went to visit them, and when I saw Vicki's face I knew something was seriously wrong. I gave her a hug and a kiss, and she said she had to go to the airport to get her uncle. I said, 'I am coming with you,' and she said okay . . .

On the way there she had a little cry and told me exactly what had happened. I was very upset by this and tried to absorb everything. I kept quiet for a few minutes, and then I said, 'Sweetheart, I know you are in the middle of a disaster. I know your life is "over" in your head, and it is the "end of the world", but you know what? You don't know how lucky you are.'

She looked at me in a puzzled manner, wondering what on earth I could possibly be talking about. I then said, 'Breaking up a relationship is never a happy occasion, but let's find the positives out of this.' She frowned like she was wondering what positives can come out of breaking up a relationship.

'I know', I said, 'that he has many good qualities, but unfortunately the bad ones have taken over. He has suddenly realised that he cannot take responsibility to be a husband. He told you at that moment that his beautiful boat has a hole in it. My question is, why would you want to get on that boat? He suddenly told you that you have many faults. If that was true and he avoided discussing it with you all this time, then he has a communication problem.'

I continued, 'If it is not true, then he is a liar, so why trust the "captain"? In my opinion *you are a lucky girl for spotting the hole on that boat before you made a commitment to take your life's journey on it.*

It is better to cry for a week or two now rather than cry for the rest of your life, not knowing when you will sink. In some cases it's worth repairing the "hole" if it had happened halfway through the journey, but in this case you haven't even started. The only thing Bappoo can say is, *"Galos, galos o shiros mas, evkigen halaziaris."'*

Moral
If you don't get to know one properly, you can have unpleasant surprises.

Before you get on a boat for your life's journey, don't only look at the shape and colour of the boat; check for holes. Look at the inner beauty.

8. Gamila glanni sto Bendagomon.
8. Καμήλα κλάννει στο Πεντάκωμο.
8. Camel farts in Bendagomo (village).

Meaning
Here I am talking to you, and it has the same effect as if a camel farts, coming out the other ear. In other words, you didn't hear a word I said.

Used
Used when you talk to one but what you say goes through one ear and out the other.

Example
Chris was trying to explain to his mum how computers work. She had absolutely no idea about computers and didn't understand what Chris was talking about. He asked her questions, but she just looked at him, completely lost. He then yelled, 'I am talking to you and you, *gamila glanni sto Bendagomon.*'

Moral
It's pointless talking if you don't get the attention.

9. Gatse yare psofa osti na vki drifillin.
9. Κάτσε γάρε ψώφα όστι να φκεί το τριφύλλι.
9. Sit and die, donkey, until the clover grows.

Yannaros (big John) with his donkey

Meaning
The donkey has to wait a very long time for the clover to grow so it can eat.

Used
Used when one is told to wait a very long time for something of necessity and urgency.

Example
Elizabeth went to the dental hospital in agony with toothache. She was given painkillers and was told that the earliest she could

be seen by a dentist was after eight months. She then said, 'It won't be necessary to see a doctor by then because my tooth will be rotten.' Bappoo then said, *'Gatse yare psofa osti na vki drifillin.'*

Moral
Seek alternative methods, or improvise if you can't wait.

*10. Gitakse din gambooran soo, brin na bis yia don **a**llon.*

10. Κοίταξε την καμπούρα σου πρν να πεις για τον άλλον.

10. Look at your own hump before you criticise others.

Meaning

One with obvious imperfections cannot mock another.

Used

Used when one that's imperfect ironically gossips about the imperfections of others.

Example

Zavos has a limp and he can't walk straight, yet when he sees someone else with a little imperfection he makes a mocking comment. That is when you say to him, *'Gitakse din gambooran soo, brin na bis yia don **a**llon.'*

Moral

Look at your own faults before you criticise others.

11. Goronos goronoo, mmadin enivgalli.
11. Κόρονος κορόνου αμμάτιν εν ηφκάλλει.
11. One magpie doesn't harm another.

Meaning
Magpies don't hurt each other but protect each other.

Used
Used when people of same beliefs, interests, or race stick together, support one another, and cover up for one another.

Example
A government minister was accused of using taxpayers' money for personal benefit. When other party members were scrutinised by the media, they showed symptoms of memory loss and tried to cover up for each other.

Then I said, '*Goronos goronoo, mmadin enivgalli.*'

Moral
People that have common interests or beliefs stick together.

12. Gootshia je gologasin, enan dobon en na basin.
12. Κουτσιά τζαι κολοκάσι έναν τόπον εννά πάσι.
12. Broad beans and taro are going into the same place.

Meaning
Broad beans and taro will fill my stomach, and that's all I am interested in.

Used
Used when one eats a variety of food in no particular order, the main objective being to fill one's empty stomach.

Example
This proverb was used mainly by poor people that did not have many food choices and had to eat whatever was available, or given to them – a bit of this, a bit of that, and a bit of leftover from the previous day.

They didn't worry about what they ate or with what, as long as they filled their stomach. That's why they say, *'Gootshia je gologasin, enan dobon en na basin.'*

Moral
Availability of food is more important than the way is served or consumed.

H

1. Horevke jira Maroo, ma'shie jenian doo moroo.
1. Χόρευκε τζυρά Μαρού μα' σιε τζ' έγνοιαν του μωρού.
1. You can dance, Mrs Marou, but keep an eye on the baby too.

Irene belly dancing, 1998

Meaning
You can dance, Mrs Marou, but don't forget that your main task is to look after the baby.

Used
Used as a reminder when one tends to forget one's main task and sidetracks.

Example

Tammy was in charge of the stall at the exhibition. Every time her boss visited the show she was not there because she was chatting with all the reps from the neighbouring stalls. Then the boss said to her, '*Horevke jira Maroo, mashe jenian doo moroo.*'

Moral

Always remember your main task.

II

1. I Athina se voitha, ma vale J'esoo shierin.
1. Η Αθηνά σε βοηθά, μα βαλε τζαι εσού σιηεριν.
1. Goddess Athena helps you, if you use your hands.

Ancient Greek: **Sin** Athen**a** ke h**i**ra k**i**ni

Meaning
Along with Athena move your hands too.

Used
Used when one sits idle doing nothing to solve a problem and expects others, or God, to do it.

Example
This is a story from the Greek mythology about a delivery man that had his wagon wheel bogged down in the mud and couldn't move it. A priest was passing by and saw him on the side of the road, down on his knees praying to Goddess Athena to get his wagon unstuck.

Seeing the priest, the disgruntled man complained that Athena wasn't helping him, and he didn't know what to do.

The priest smiled and said, 'Along with Athena use your hands too. *I Athin**a** se voith**a**, ma vale J'es**oo** shierin.*'

There is a difference between asking for help to do something and asking one to do it for you while you watch.

Moral
The earlier you take charge of your life, the better.

The Thirty-Five-Year-Old 'Teenagers'
That Live with Mum and Dad

There are many thirty-five-, or even forty-year-old people who still live with their parents.

Most of the parents, particularly the southern Europeans, not only don't encourage them to move out and take control of their own lives but think that it is their obligation to take care of them.

They treat them like kings, especially the boys. Mum does everything for them. Of course, they mean well and do it because they love them, but perhaps, they don't know how much harm they could be doing to them.

There are some exceptions, like when they are studying or working on a plan to save money to buy their own dwelling, but otherwise, most of these thirty-fivers don't want to move out or get married and be independent. Why should they? The parents create such a comfort zone for them that they don't want to move out. As a result, most of these 'kids' don't learn how to be independent and find it very hard to take control of their own life later on.

Even if they meet a partner and decide to get married and move out, the majority of them expect mum's service from their spouse which, of course, doesn't happen in most cases. The boys, mainly, find it difficult to cope without mum, and this can cause a major problem in their relationship. This is the harm that I was talking about.

I remember years ago in the early 1970s, in a jungle in South Africa about three hours' north of Johannesburg, I had a friend who was a ninety-eight-year-old retired Afrikaner doctor. He lived with his eighty-year-old son, also a doctor.

The senior was an exceptionally knowledgeable and wise man, who taught me a few things. They both lived a very natural and simple life, and we had many interesting conversations.

The following story was one of them, and it has come to my mind as we are on the subject of mum's boys.

Once there was a little Chinese girl who was spending the weekend on her grandfather's silk farm. She walked down the shed's aisle, browsing through all the silk cocoons spread on racks and ready to hatch. As she was walking through, she noticed one of them moving. She stopped and had a closer look, and suddenly her eyes popped out as she saw a little head rising out of the cocoon; she was astonished. Open-mouthed, she watched a tiny little butterfly trying to rip through the tough skin of the cocoon to free herself.

This went on for a few minutes, and the tiny butterfly was still battling to rip through. The little girl felt so sorry for it that she took a small knife and ripped the hole larger to help the butterfly come out.

Her grandfather was sitting nearby watching what she was doing and shook his head in disagreement.

'Why, Grandfather, what have I done wrong?' she asked.

'Wait a minute and you will see,' he replied.

The butterfly fell out through the enlarged opening, tried to stand on its feet and to open its wings, but was extremely weak and couldn't do it.

Unfortunately, she didn't have the strength to fight any longer; she gave up, and a few minutes later she died.

The little girl looked at her granddad with tears in her eyes and asked, 'Why, Grandfather? Why?'

'Because, sweetheart,' he replied, 'the pushing and the struggle to come out of the cocoon is a very important part of life. It is what pushes the blood through the veins to give the strength that's needed in order to survive and be strong and healthy, physically and mentally. You just have interfered with Mother Nature's job.'

The same applies to humans. When we 'rip open' our kid's cocoon, we bypass nature. We can only nurture them while they are developing in our care, but once they begin the process of coming out, they should be on their own. They need to get out to experience and go through the natural process of being adults. They need to take charge of their own life, to make mistakes and learn by them, and also to exercise their sense of survival and become stronger and wiser. Parents will not be around forever.

2. *I gooza bai bolles fores stin vrisin, amma gabode spazi.*
2. Η κούζα πάει πολλές φορές στη βρύσην, αμμά κάποτε σπάζει.
2. The pot goes to the fountain many times, but one day it smashes.

Water pot (*gooza*)

Meaning

It doesn't matter how well you look after a fragile object; when you use it frequently, one day it will break.

Used

Used when one gets away with dangerous or risky actions sometimes but eventually gets caught.

Example
My Friend Spiro's Driving (Joke)

Last time I went to Cyprus I caught a taxi to go to my uncle's house in Kiti. The taxi driver had Greek music playing *Zeibekika* and asked me where I was coming from. I said, 'Australia.' He said, 'You kangaroos are loaded, aren't you?' I said, 'Yes. That's why I have two suitcases.' As we approached an intersection with red lights, he didn't show any signs of slowing down. Holding on to the front seat, I watched him in horror as he went through the red lights. I yelled at him, 'What the hell are you doing?' He said, 'Don't worry, my friend Spiro does that all the time.'

'I don't give a damn about your friend Spiro! I don't want to be killed,' I said very angrily. As we come to the next intersection, the same thing happened, big commotion. His answer was again, 'Don't worry. You kangaroos are too scared. My friend Spiro does it all the time.'

As we approached the next intersection, I braced myself, getting ready for the next red light. I was happy to see that they changed to green, but then that idiot stopped. I said, 'Why you stopped at green?'

He replied, 'Just give me a minute to check if my friend Spiro is coming.' I never caught a taxi again, and Bappoo said, '*I gooza bai bolles fores stin vrisin, amma gabode spazi.*'

Moral
All fragile or dangerous things have an expiry date.

3. I bolli thoolia droi don afendin.
3. Η πολλή δουλειά τρώει τον αφέντην.
3. Too much work can kill you.

Meaning
When you overwork your body, it can kill you.

Used
Used when one works too hard and doesn't take a break.

Example
An uncle had a grocery shop that opened from 4 a.m. to 9 p.m., 7 days a week, 364.5 days a year. He worked with his family for more than forty years like that. He made a lot of money, but he didn't even have time to retire. When he did, he was too ill to enjoy his money.

That's when Bappoo says, *'I bolli thoolia droi don afendin.'*

Moral
Work to live, not live to work.

*4. **I**vres don **a**yion soo, n'**a**psis do jerin soo.*
4. Ηβρες τον άγιον σου ν' άψεις το τζερί σου.
4. You found your saint to light your candle.

Meaning
When Greek Orthodox people worship a saint, they usually light a candle and place it in a candle holder in front of the icon.

Metaphorically, it means, you found the one that's smarter than you and put you in your place.

Used
Used when you are smart to someone who easily outsmarts you and puts you in an embarrassing situation.

Example
Mahatma Gandhi was known for his eloquence, and when he was studying at the university, one of his lecturers Mr Bradley, hated him for that.

One day Gandhi went down to the lunch room, picked up his lunch, and sat next to him. Mr Bradley gave him a dirty look and quite rudely said, 'Don't you know that pigs and birds don't sit together?'

Gandhi thought for a minute, stood up, picked up his tray, and said, 'Okay sir, I will fly away.'

That's when Bappoo can say to Mr Bradley, *'**I**vres don **a**yion soo, n**a**psis do jerin soo.'*

Moral
Don't challenge people if you don't know their capabilities.

5. I alooboo efaen da gadoorimena dis.
5. Η αλουπού έφαεν τα κατουρημένα της.
5. The fox ate what she pissed on.

Similar to English version: Spitting against the wind.

Meaning
When you do the wrong thing, it will come back to you.

Used
Used when someone does the wrong thing by others, and when their circumstances change, they go back crawling in shame.

Example
The Fox and the Apricots

A fox found an apricot tree in the desert with all its fruit fallen to the ground. She ate and ate until she was so full, she couldn't eat any more.

Because she was selfish and didn't want anyone else to eat the fruit, she urinated all over the rest of the apricots, laughing that the others would eat the pissed-on ones. The next day she got hungry again, and because it was only one tree in the area, she had no choice but to go back to it.

She walked around the tree with her tail between her legs, looked and looked, trying to find any apricots without any urine on them, but no luck. She then picked up one, closed her eyes, and said, 'I am sure this is clean and there is no urine on it,' and ate it.

She then repeated the same thing until she ate them all. Bappoo then said, '*I alooboo efaen da gadoorimena dis.*'

Moral
What goes around comes around.

6. *I alooboo ston ibnon dis ethhoren bedinarga.*
6. Η αλουπού στον ύπνον της εθώρεν πετεινάρκα.
6. The fox was dreaming of chickens.

Meaning
The fox is known to have a good appetite for chickens as her favourite meal, and that's why she always dreams of chickens when hungry.

Used
Used when one wishes that one's desire become reality.

Example
Grandpa had no teeth, but he loved rusks. Every time he went in the supermarket and saw them, he would say, 'I wish I could eat some of these rusks.' Grandma then would say, *'I alooboo ston ibnon dis ethhoren bedinarga.'*

Moral
Stop day dreaming and face reality.

7. I kali mera fenede boo do broin.
7. Η καλή μέρα φαίνεται που το πρωί.
7. The fine day shows from the morning.

Meaning
I guess this mainly applies to countries like southern Europe where the weather is stable and more predictable. This proverb was actually used by the farmers to decide whether they are going to work on the field or not, as the main decisive factor was always the weather. If the day looked bad from the start, it was not likely to improve.

Used
Used when you work on a project and whatever could go wrong goes wrong.

Example
The potato-farmer arranged for Monday morning to start potato-picking. He prepared the tractor with the ploughers, the pickers, and the packers.

At seven o'clock they started with half of the pickers not turning up.

The containers hadn't been delivered, so the packers couldn't do their work, and on top of everything else the tractor broke down. The farmer then said, *'I gali mera fenede boo do broi.'*

Moral
Before you commence work on a project, consider all aspects.

***8.** Iban doo bell**oo** na shi**e**si, J**e**vkalen je d**a**ndera doo.*
8. Είπαν του πελλού να σιέσει τζ'
έφκαλεν τζαι τ' άντερα του.
8. They told a fool to have a shit,
and he pushed his intestines out.

Meaning
They asked a fool to do something, and he went overboard.

Used
Used when you instruct an unqualified person to do something and he/she overdoes it.

Example
When you ask someone to fill a bottle with oil and they overfill it and make a mess. This is when you say, *'Iban doo belloo na shesi je evgalen je ta andera doo.'*

Moral
Deal with sensible people.

9. Iben o yaros doo bedinoo, jefala.
9. Είπεν ο γάρος του πετεινού τζεφάλα.
9. The donkey called the rooster big-headed.

Meaning
The donkey is known to have a big head, and yet he tried to ridicule the rooster by calling him big-headed.

Metaphorically, it means that one with an imperfection mocks one who is normal. (Even though the donkey's head is in proportion with his body, in this case it is considered to be extra-large.)

Used
Used when one has an obvious imperfection and yet tries to ridicule others.

Example
Rene was a middle-aged lady, who was always trying to look her best. She was a bit chubby, but beautiful. One day she walked in

the hall, where the oldies had a gathering, and a very fat old lady said to her, 'Oh my God, Rene, you put on a lot of weight!' Rene gave her a dirty look and said, **'*I*ben o *y*aros doo bedin*oo*,** *jefala.*'

Moral

Before you ridicule or criticise others, look at your own imperfections.

10. I ylossa cokkala then ehi je cokkala tsakkizi.
10. Η γλώσσα κόκκαλα δεν έχει τζαι κόκκαλα τσακκίζει.
10. The tongue has no bones, but crushes bones.

Meaning
Even though the tongue doesn't have bones, it is powerful enough to cause a lot of damage.

Used
Used when someone bad-mouths others, causing them problems and damaging their reputation.

Example
Elli is an open and happy bubbly lady that split up with her husband after years of marriage, because some idiot by the name Johnnie told his mates in the caffenio that she was having an affair. Obviously, any girl that talks to a man, for him it appears to be having sex. His mates, having lower mentality than him, spread the word very fast until it reached Elli's husband's ears. The rest is history.

When I heard about it, I shook my head and remembered Bappoos words:

'I ylossa cokkala then ehi je cokkala tsakkizi.'

Moral
Think before you spread rumours that could harm others.

11. I gali loargasmi gamnoon doos galoos filoos.
11. Οι καλοί λοαρκασμοί κάμνουν τους καλούς φίλους.
11. Good agreements make good friends.

Meaning
Any dealings you do ensure that they are transparent and understood by all parties involved and documented so there will be no arguments later.

Used
Used when a friendship is damaged due to lack of transparent and proper written agreements.

Example
The Handshake (True story**)**

My grandfather Dimitros always spoke to me about handshakes and how important it was to honour your word. I believe in that strongly, and it was always my principle in business. A few of my friends knew that, and they took advantage of me, my knowledge, and my hard work. They promised me the world to do business with me, one way or another, and I agreed with a handshake. I considered a handshake to be my signature, so I didn't worry about written agreements. Many times I left it to their discretion, but then I realised that greediness makes people ignore handshakes, gives them selective memory, and destroys friendships. At the end, I lost a lot of money and 'friends' and I was very disappointed. I realised that a handshake was enough years ago when everyone valued it. I came to realise now that handshakes don't mean anything any more and only written agreements count. Bappoo said, *'I gali loargasmi gamnoon doos galoos filoos.'*

Moral

Make documented agreements to protect your interest and your friendship.

12. I niffi brin na yennithi dis bethheras dis miazi.
12. Η νύμφη πριν να γεννίθεί της πεθθεράς ημοιάζει.
12. The bride looks like her mother-in-law before she is even born.

My mother Christalleni with her daughter-in-law, Yeoryia. 1983.

Meaning

Usually the son-in-law or daughter-in-law has a lot of similarities with one of their in-laws to the point that some people say that they take after them before they are even born.

Used

Used when the bride or groom show that they have a lot in common with one of their in-laws.

Example
(True story)

My sister-in-law, Yeoryoolla, had a lot in common with her mother-in-law, to the point that many thought they were mother and daughter. They had a lot in common and loved each other very much. They were an ideal case of *'I niffi brin na yennithi dis bethheras dis miazi'.*

Moral
Love your mother-in-law to have a happy marriage.

***13.** Irtan da **a**rka na vgaloon da **i**mera.*
13. Ηρταν τ' άρκα να φκάλουν τα ήμερα.
13. The feral came and chased the domestic.

Meaning
The ones that don't belong came to remove the ones that belong.

Used
Used when others arrogantly take over one's property and make themselves at home.

Example
During the hunting season many hunters go to the country sites looking for hares, particularly up on the mountains. There are many private properties that are not fenced off, and the hunters

take advantage of it and walk through, causing damage to the crops. The farmers complain, but nobody takes any notice. One day Andrikko caught six of them stealing his mandarins by the bag loads and destroying his *louvana* (lentils). He yelled at them to get out, and they swore at him and said arrogantly, 'Kalan Seior, we picked a couple of mandarins, so what?'

He then said, 'A couple? I don't believe it. *Irtan da arka na vgaloon da imera.*'

Moral
Respect the property of others.

14. *Inda'nemos efisisen je'feresse thagado.*
14. Ηντ' άνεμος εφύσησεν τζ' έφερε σε δακάτω.
14. What wind blew you our way?

Meaning
What brought you here all of a sudden?

Used
Used as a sarcastic remark when an unexpected and rare visitor shows up.

Example
When an old friend or a relative, or a candidate for the council, pays you an unexpected visit after a long time, then you say, '*Inda anemos efisisen je eferesse thagado?*'

Moral
When you have unexpectedly rare visitors, most probably they are after something.

*15. I ab**a**ndisi doo bell**oo** en i siob**i**.*
15. Η απάντηση του πέλλού εν η σιωπή.
15. Silence is the best way to deal with an idiot.

Meaning
When you are challenged by an idiot, ignoring him is the best policy.

Used
Used in an effort to avoid confrontation with idiots.

Example
I went to the airport one day, and I was looking for a parking spot. I saw a car ready to drive out, and I waited with my indicator on. As soon as the other car drove out, some idiot came flying from behind and took my spot. I looked at him and saw that he stuck his finger up and I realised that I wasn't dealing with a normal person and I drove off. I remembered what Bappoo said, '*I ab**a**ndisi doo bell**oo** en i siob**i**.*'

Moral
Silence is the best policy when you deal with idiots.

16. I bandria ellahion.
16. Η παντρειά ε'λλαχείον.
16. Marriage is a lottery.

Meaning
Marriage is like buying a lottery ticket. Either you are lucky and find the right person, or you are not.

Used
A comment used to express belief in luck when it concerns marriage.

Example
Julia divorced her husband because he was a compulsive gambler and was never home. He was in bad mood when he was home, and they were constantly arguing. Her father said to me very sadly, *'I bandria ine lahion* – If you win, you win.'

Moral
Hope for the best.

To have a successful marriage, look for a compatible person, one that's understanding, compromising, respectful, caring, and trusting. (This is winning the lottery.)

The Husband with a Rare Disease (Joke)

This reminds me of the story of my late friend Russell. His wife took him to the doctor for a check-up because he was complaining about anything and everything.

The doctor gave him a thorough, one-hour check-up and was taking notes. When he finished, he frowned and asked Russell to step outside because he wanted to talk to his wife alone. That made Russell very concerned, but he went outside and closed the door. Then the doctor sat next to Russell's wife and looked at her. She asked if there was something wrong.

He nodded affirmatively and said, 'I am sorry, but your husband suffers from a rare depression, and he doesn't have much time left. There is a chance to overcome the problem, though, and get better, but it would require a lot of effort on your behalf.'

She said, 'What? What can I do, Doctor?'

'You need to treat him like a baby, buy him whatever he wants, make him breakfast every morning with a massage, make him lunch with a massage, dinner with a massage every day. Give him the remote control of the TV and give him sex whenever he wants it. The tender love and care might improve his condition.'

She then got up, thanked the doctor, and left. She went straight to her husband and gave him a big hug with tears in her eyes.

On the way to the car he made a few attempts to ask what the doctor said, but she couldn't talk. On the way home he asked her again what the doctor said, and she just looked at him.

He then said, 'The doctor said I am going to die, didn't he?'

After a short pause she answered, 'Yes, dear.'

17. I azoola an idan booza, idan na booziasi o kosmos oolos.
17. Η αζουλα αν ηταν πουζα ηταν να πουζιασει ο κοσμος ουλλος.
17. If jealousy was hernia, the whole world would have had hernia.

Meaning
Everyone in the world has some degree of jealousy.

Used
It is used to express your disappointment when others copy you due to jealousy.

Example
The Two Jealous Brothers-in-Law

Costas and Vasilis married two sisters. Costa was a policeman, and Vasilis was a teacher. They were so jealous and competitive of each other that whatever one did, the other had to do better.

Costas built a house in the village. Vasilios built a double-storeyed house in the village. Costas used mosaics for the front stairs. Vasilios used granite for the front stairs. Costas then hired a jackhammer and broke all the mosaic tiles and replaced them with marble from Italy to be better.

Their father-in-law then said, *'I azoola an idan booza, idan na booziasi o kosmos oolos.'*

Having more than others doesn't make one a better person.

Moral
When one shows jealousy, it is an admission of one looking up to you.

J

1. Ji boo grazoon bolli bedini argi na ksimerosi.
1. Τζίει που κράζουσιν πολλοί πετεινοί αρκεί να ξημερώσει.
1. Too many roosters delay the dawn.

English version: Too many cooks spoil the broth.

Meaning
When too many roosters crow at different times, you don't know who is right.

Used
Used when too many bosses make decisions but no one is in charge to coordinate actions.

Example
Efficiency and Productivity

The new manager of a company conducted a four-week study to establish the reasons why productivity was so low. In no time he established that the main reason was that too many unqualified managers or relatives were giving uncoordinated orders and there was no control. He then called a meeting and told everyone that there would be a lot of changes in the business to increase efficiency and productivity. He pointed out all the problems and the proposed solutions.

He then set boundaries in each department, appointed a foreman in each one, and instructed them all to only report to him. He improved communication methods, and the results were unbelievable. That's where Bappoo says, *'Ji boo grazoon bolli bedini argi na ksimerosi.'*

Moral
There should only be one boss making decisions.

2. Jiame bou ise imoon, je thame boo ime enna'rtis.
2. Τζιαμέ που είσαι ήμουν τζιαι δαμέ που είμαι εν νάρτεις.
2. Where you are I have been, and where I am you will be.

My mother-in-law, Angeloo Odyssea Ioannou, surrounded by her children in the last days of her life, 2009

Meaning
This is a reminder to the young that they will get old one day as well.

Used
Used when younger people disregard, disrespect, or even harass their elders.

Example
I remember when my mother was looking after her parents and her in-laws, four old people one after the other, over a period of fifteen years.

She never complained and always felt that it was her duty to look after them. Of course, those days there were no facilities or government assistance that we have today, and it was much more difficult for the old and the carers.

She used to tell me stories about the good and the bad, about how the human cycle goes. How we are born as babies, become adults, then middle aged, then older, and back to babies again, some worse than others, some lucky enough to be able to look after themselves.

She said that we shouldn't forget that when we are new parents we have an obligation to look after our babies at any cost and under any circumstances with no excuses. Consequently, when the children become adults and the adults become 'babies', in my books, any fair person would understand that it's a moral obligation to do the same. We are all going to be in that position one day; that's life. Of course, there are exemptions. If it's impossible to do it ourselves due to work or any other commitments, or reasons beyond our control, then we can make sure that we place them in good care, like we would have done with our babies.

Our children will see how we look after our oldies and learn by example. If we find excuses, our children will find excuses.

Moral
It's a moral obligation for any child to return the care to the parents.

3. *Jinos pap**as**, jinos dad**as**.*
3. Τζιείνος παπάς, τζιείνος τατάς.
3. He is the priest and the godfather.

Meaning
When the priest that baptises the baby is also the godfather, he can make all the decisions.

Used
Used when one in authority holds more than one office and has full autonomy.

Example
My Business Trip to Botswana (True story)

In 1972, I drove with my friend Freddy from Johannesburg to Botswana, a small town just inside the border. There was a huge shortage of tomatoes then, so we visited the high commissioner to obtain an import permit for tomatoes to Botswana from South Africa.

We notified the reception that he was expecting us, and the receptionist showed us to his office. We walked in and stood in front of his desk, said good morning, and stood there waiting.

He had his feet on top of his desk, his face in an open newspaper, and he didn't even acknowledge us.

We stood there for ten minutes, waiting for him to respond to our greetings. I started to feel a bit uneasy, and Freddy was elbowing me to keep quiet.

We waited for another ten minutes and started to get a bit nervous. I think he picked up on our body language; he took a peek and asked if there was a problem.

I said, 'Sorry, but we are not used to doing business this way.'

'Well,' he said, 'if you want to do business with me, you have to do it my way. You have to make me happy.'

'Well,' I said, 'can we get the permit?'

He said, 'Can you afford it?'

I asked, 'How much?'

He replied, 'It depends how much money you have.'

I paused for a minute and then said I wanted to talk to his superior.

He then put the newspaper down and, with a big smile on his face, replied,

'I am my superior, *and* the chief of police.'

I looked at my friend, and we both walked out, never to return there again.

I said, 'You can't win, *jinos papas, jinos dadas.*'

Moral
When you deal with multi-authority, you can't win.

4. Jiloon davgon me din manavellan.
4. Τζιυλούν τ' αυκόν με την μαναβέλλαν.
4. They roll an egg with a beam.

Similar to English version:
Using a sledgehammer to crack a walnut.

Meaning
They use a whole beam to push a little object such as an egg.

Used
Used when one wrongly uses gigantic tools or methods not proportional to the object or project.

Example
Twenty council workers, a heavy bulldozer, a truck, and two tractors came to my street to fix a little pothole for half a day. Bappoo then said, '*Jiloon davgon me din manavellan.*'

Moral
Use the correct tool for the job.

5. *Jinos bon se kseri, agriva se yorazi.*
5. Τζείνος πον σε ξέρει, ακριβά σε γοράζει.
5. Who doesn't know you, buys you expensive.

Meaning
You appear to be very good, and many people would think you are worth a lot of money, until they get to know who you really are.

Used
It's used to warn a smooth-talker that only people that don't know one would deal with one.

Example
Tony is a very sweet young man, who is always very polite and respectful. He is a salesman and is such a sweet-talker that one day I witnessed a sale where he lied to the customer in order to make the sale. Afterwards I said to him, *'Jinos bon se kseri, agriva se yorazi.'*

Moral
Beware of the sly ones

K

Ksenos golos oson thelis htiba.
Ξένος κώλος όσο θέλεις χτύπα
Someone else's buttock, smack as much as you like.

Meaning
Because it is someone else's bum, you don't care if others smack it.

Used
Used as an objection to misusing the property of others.

Example
When you don't bother turning off the lights after you walk out of the room, or when you have the heater on full blast, even in good weather, simply because you are a guest and you don't pay the bills, Bappoo says, '*Ksenos golos oson thelis htiba.*'

Moral
Respect the property of other's particularly when it is in your care.

L

*1. **Lamne broin** is din **thoolian** je an**o**ras is do sp**i**din.*
1. Λάμνε πρωίν εις τη δουλειά τζ' ανώρας εις το σπίτι.
1. Work early in the morning and go home early.

Meaning
The farmers in the village usually start working just before sunrise so they can finish and go home early. They believe that the early hours of the morning are the most productive and beneficial physically and mentally, particularly in hot days.

Used
It's used to encourage one to start working early and to finish early.

Example
Christo was a cucumber farmer, but he had one problem. He was not an early riser. He used to wake up late and go to work at ten o'clock. He was copping the heat of summer, and also, by the time he took his cucumbers to the market, everyone else was sold out.

His grandfather said to him, *'Lamne broin is din thoolian je anoras is do spidin.'* Then he tried it, and he realised what he was doing wrong.

Moral
Early start, productive day.

2. Lamne mavroirevke.
2. Λάμνε μαυροϋρεφκε
2. Go surging in the dark.

English version: Go to hell.

Meaning
Go and look for the answer somewhere that you can't see anything.

Used
It's used to express one's anger when the person involved asks a question.

Example
Tina asked her sister to lend her one of her blouses, because she was going on a date with a boy she just met. Her sister said no, and they had a heated argument that made Tina very upset. She decided to wear something else anyway.

On the way out her sister asked her where she was going, and Tina quite angrily replied, '*Lamne mavroirevke.*'

Moral
Release some steam without swearing.

3. Lali do i garkia do.
3. Λαλεί το η καρκιά του.
3. He's got guts.

Meaning
One is not afraid of anything.

Used
It's used to demonstrate that one has no fear in doing something.

Example (True story)
Kelly the Pit Bull

My Italian friend Giuseppe was a hunter, and his dog Kelly, a pit bull, was his right hand when he went pig shooting. She was a gutsy little dog that wouldn't take no for an answer when she was attacking a pig.

One time, she came face to face with a huge boar with his tusks sticking out of his mouth, and as Kelly was attacking him, he ripped her guts open, but she still kept on going back despite Giuseppe's attempts to stop her.

I said, *'Lali do i garkia doo,'* and Giuseppe explained to me that pit bulls have a lot of guts but no brains to protect themselves.

So what Giuseppe did was to cross Kelly with a Rottweiler, which is very intelligent dog, to boost the pit bull's intelligence and judgement. The results where unbelievable.

Moral
Be brave but not stupid.

4. Libi o Martis boo din saracosdin?
4. Λείπει ο Μάρτης που τη Σαρακοστήν.
4. Is March ever absent from Lent?

Meaning

Even though the date changes for the Greek Orthodox Lent, it always falls around March.

Used

Used as a remark when you keep meeting the same person in every event you attend.

Example

Chris loves going to all religious festivities on saints' name days and so does George. The last one was Theofania, when the bishop throws the cross in the sea from the pier, and all the youngsters dive in to collect it and be blessed. That day, Chris walked in, and there was George, buying *lokoumathes* (Greek doughnuts). As soon as George saw him he said, *'Libi o Martis boo din saracosdin?'*

Moral

It's healthy to get out and enjoy yourself and be happy.

5. Libi o gattos je i bondiji horevgoon.
5. Λείπει ο κάττος τζαι οι ποντιτζιοί χορεύκουν.
5. The mice are dancing while the cat is away.

Meaning
When the boss is away, everyone is happy because they can relax.

Used
Used when everyone takes advantage of the boss's absence and slug off.

Example
The manager of a blinds manufacturer went away on business, and the workers slacked off, walking around and taking it easy. A regular customer came to pick up something and said, '*Libi o gattos je i bondiji horevgoon.*'

Moral
Most employees need constant supervision.

6. Loargazoosin horis don ksenothohon.
6. Λοαρκάζουσιν χωρίς τον ξενοδόχο.
6. Making plans without the host.

Meaning

They are making plans to do something in the hotel, and the hotelier has not been consulted.

Used

It's used to highlight the fact that there is no point in planning without the approval of the authorities.

Example

The kids are organising with their friends to have a party at Benny's place. Their mum overhears the conversation from the kitchen and asks if Benny's dad knows about it. They say no.

Mum then says, '*Loargazoosin horis don ksenothohon.*'

Moral

Obtain appropriate permits prior to commencement.

M

1. Ma nomizis bos en do hanin doo Panjaroo?
1. Μα νομίζεις εν το χάνι του Ππάντζιαρου;
1. Do you think this is the Panjarou's hostel?

Meaning
The hostel of Panjarou was in Nicosia and was used by many travellers from all over Cyprus. It was open twenty-four hours a day, ready to accommodate anyone, any time they showed up seeking refuge. No rules, no appointments needed.

Used
It's used when people show lack of consideration, expecting service as they please.

Example
When the kids come home with their friends and they raid the fridge and the pantry without permission from mum or dad, that's when mum or dad will say, *'Ma nomizete bos en do hanin doo Panjaroo'?*

Moral
It is wise and polite to make prior arrangements when you need others.

> *2. Mathhe dehnin je gremmasdin is do balloojin.*
> 2. Μάθε τέχνη τζαι κρέμμαστην στο παλλούτσιν.
> 2. Learn a trade and hang it on the hook.

Meaning
It is wise to learn a trade even if you don't use it.

Keep it for a 'rainy day' as a safety net.

Used
It's used to advise the offspring about the importance of having a qualification.

Example
Costas the Electrician (True story)

My friend Costas was born in Alexandria, Egypt, in 1938. When he graduated from elementary school, he had to make the first important decision of his life. That would be what trade or profession he would go for. He loved music and had a tendency towards arts. His father wasn't very happy about it because that was not considered to be a solid money-earning job those days. He said, 'I don't care what you decide to do, but whatever it is, you have to learn a proper trade first to have as a safety net.' Like Bappoo says, '*Mathhe dehnin je gremmasdin is do balloojin.*'

Costas considered everything his father told him and followed his advice. He enrolled in a technical school to become an electrician, and after he had his certificate he also did music lessons.

In 1957 when he was 19 years old he migrated to Australia, looking for a better future. On his arrival one of his relatives helped him get a job at the glass factory making glass bottles. After working there for a short period of time, it was noticed by the management that he had some education and other skills. He was multilingual and good in maths. That would help them solve a communication problem they had with many European workers that couldn't speak English. They called him in the office one day and offered him an office position with more money, which he gladly accepted. By the time he was twenty-seven years old, he decided to get married. It was then that he realised that his responsibilities would be a lot more and started thinking. He remembered that *he had a trade hanging up on the* ballooji (hook), and he decided to use it. He got a job as a B grade electrician. There was a little problem with the Egyptian certificate, as it was not recognised in Australia as A grade. He then decided go to night school for six months while he was working, to get his A grade certificate that he needed in order to start his own business. Eventually he did; he bought a van and never looked back. He now knows the importance of what Bappoo used to say, '*Mathhe dehnin je gremmasdin is do balloojin.*'

Moral
A qualification makes you more employable

> *3. Mathhe yiero yrammada.*
> 3. Μάθε γέρο γράμματα
> 3. You can't teach an old man how to read and write.

English equivalent: You can't teach old dog new tricks.

Meaning
Old people are set in their own ways and don't want their space to be invaded.

Used
Used when one attempts to take an old person out of his/her comfort zone to teach them new things.

Example
Bappoo Nikos and His Garden (True story)

Bappoo Nikos was a healthy eighty-eight-year-old man, quite energetic for his age, and he loved spending time in his garden. It was his pride and joy, and he would get a lot of pleasure out of sharing his produce with all his friends. Planting, watering, or picking vegies – it was an occupational therapy for him and a pleasant way of passing his time. His wife was bedridden with MS, and he looked after her for a few months, before she passed away.

Losing his life partner, after sixty-five years of being together, was like he lost half of his body. He couldn't bear the pain. He would go in his garden to keep himself busy, crying and talking to himself. His garden was the only thing he had left that could keep him occupied and help him soothe his pain.

One day another disaster happened. His son came and said to him that he was going to sell the house and buy him one close to where he lived so he didn't have to travel half an hour to visit him. He said, 'Oh no, what about my garden? I need my garden. I don't need anyone to look after me. I can manage.' His son then said, 'You will meet other people, and you're also going to learn how to use a computer. Bappoo then said, 'No, I don't want to learn anything, *Mathhe yiero yrammada.*'

His son, unfortunately, didn't listen and put him in a new house that he had bought, away from his neighbours, from his garden, and from everything he loved. Four months later the old man died of sorrow and depression.

Moral
Respect old people's ways, even if you don't agree with them.

4. Mathkia boo then vleboonde efgola ksehnioonde.
4. Μάθκια που δεν βλέπουνται γλήορα ξεχνιούνται.
4. Eyes that cannot be seen are easily forgotten.

Meaning
Love can easily die out when people in love don't see each other for a long period of time.

Used
It is used as an advice that long separations can resault in loss of interest.

Example
Mario and Zaharoolla

Mario went to Australia with a working visa in order to work, make some money, and then go back and marry his girlfriend Zaharoulla. He was a photographer, and he worked with a lot of gorgeous girls. The temptations were too many and hard to resist. He fell in love with one of them, and a year later they got engaged.

After a year back in the village, Zaharoulla realised that something was wrong because their communication was getting rarer and rarer until it stopped completely. One day she received a call from Mario notifying her that he was not coming back and that he was breaking up with her. She was devastated. Her mum tried to comfort her saying that it was not the end of the world and that he was not worth the cry.

Bappoo then said, '*Mathkia boo then vleboonde efgola ksehnioonde.*'

Moral
Separation causes loss of interest

5. Me din millan mas, dianizi do vlanjin mas.
5. Με τη μίλλα μας τηανίζει το βλαντζί μας
5. Fries our liver with our own fat.

Meaning
One uses one's own fat to fry one's own liver.

Used
It's used to express one's bitterness when double injustice has been done against one.

Example
Two Tickets for the Opera (True story)

It was a summer morning in South Africa in a Johannesburg suburb called Berario. I think it was in the early 1970s during the times that the revolution against apartheid was going on, and a few *tsotsies* (bad boys) were taking advantage of it for their own benefit. It was 6 a.m., and I was ready to go to open up the shop; as I stepped out I saw my neighbours Mr and Mrs Thompson talking to the police. Mrs Thompson approached me and said that their Mercedes was stolen from the driveway, and the police are asking if I heard anything. I said, 'No, I haven't,' and left for work, until the next morning again when I was going to work and noticed the Thompsons were talking outside quite loudly. Mrs Thompson ran up to me all excited saying, 'We found the Merc.' I said, 'Where?' 'Right here in our driveway with a letter on the front seat apologising for the inconvenience, and they were embarrassed to face us. The poor people, they said they had no choice because the husband had to rush his pregnant wife to the hospital to have the baby.

'They said in the letter that in order to show their appreciation they left two tickets for the last show of the opera on Saturday commencing at 10 p.m. and here they are,' Mrs Thompson said, waving the tickets in front of my face. 'And, by the way,' she said, 'it's a boy.'

I said, 'Well done, are you going to the theatre?'

She replied, 'I love opera, and I wouldn't miss it for anything.'

Saturday came, and Mr and Mrs Thompson went off at 9.30 p.m. to their favourite opera show. They loved the show so much, and on the way home, Mrs Thompson said, 'Wasn't sweet of them to give us the tickets tonight, darling? I wish I had their address to buy the baby a present.'

They got home about 12.30 a.m., after midnight, and Mr Thompson noticed that their big van was missing from where it was parked. He rushed inside to call the police and found the front door was open. He then realised they had been robbed. He turned the light on, and the house was completely empty. Everything was gone, including the chandeliers from the ceiling. 'Obviously the robbers knew what time the show finishes, and they had lots of time,' the detective said. 'That's why they gave you the opera tickets.' Mr Thompson burst out laughing, and when the detective looked at him frowning, he said, 'Sorry, Officer, but my wife wanted to buy the baby a present.' Then the officer said, 'They used your van to rob your house.'

That's when Bappoo says, *'Me din millan mas, dianizi do vlanjin mas.'*

Moral
Beware of strangers bearing gifts.

6. *Me don thki*a*olon na tho, me don stavr*o*n moo na g*a*mo.*
6. Με τον δκιάολον να δω, με τον σταυρό μου να κάμω.
6. Neither the devil to see, nor the sign of the cross to do.

Meaning
I am neither interested to see the devil nor to get rid of it.

The Greek Orthodox believe that in the presence of the devil, all you have to do is the sign of a cross, and the devil will go away.

Used
Used when one is not interested either in the problem or in the solution.

Example
Nikos was trying to sell me a computer.

I said, 'I am not interested, because I don't even know how to use it.'

He said he could arrange to send me to computer classes.

I said, 'No, I am not interested in buying a computer or learning how to use it.' He insisted and I said, 'I am not interested, *me don thkiaolon na tho, me don stavron moo na gamo.*'

Moral
Respect other people's wishes.

> *7. Me don noon do gamni bairamin.*
> 7. Με τον νουν του κάμνει παϊράμι.
> 7. He is celebrating Ramadan in his own mind.

Meaning
One celebrates Ramadan whenever one remembers, and talks nonsense.

Used
Used when one entertains thoughts or expresses wishes that cannot become reality or cannot be taken seriously.

Example
Manoli said that he was going to build a swimming pool with a bar in it and have a huge BBQ area and a huge pergola. His wife, who knew their finances, said, *'Me don noon do gamni bairamin.'*

Moral
Face reality.

*8. Men biannis do psoomin boo do stoman
don bethkion doo belecanoo.*
8. Μεν πιάννεις το ψουμί που το στόμα
των παιδκιών του πελεκάνου.
8. Do not take the bread from the mouths
of the carpenter's children.

Meaning
A plumber doing the carpenter's job is stealing the food from a carpenter's table.

Used
Used when a tradesperson steals the work of another of different trade.

Example
Chris the electrician needed tiles in his newly renovated bathroom. Instead of calling Sotiri the tiler to do it, he did it himself. That's taking the food from the tiler's kids' mouths. Their hourly rate could be the same, but the electrician took four hours longer to do the tiling, because he was not an expert. If the electrician had spent all that time doing electrical work, he would have made more money than he saved doing tiling anyway. That's why it's said, '*Men biannis do psoomin boo do stoman don bethkion doo belecanoo.*'

Moral
Stick to your own trade.

9. Me da millo sfonjismada thheloon na gamoon bittes.
9. Με τα μιλλοσφοντσίσματα θέλουν να κάμουν πίττες.
9. They want to make pita bread from an oily rag.

Cypriot bishies

Meaning
That one is so tight with money that he/she tries to squeeze oil from an oily rag to make pita bread.

Used
Used when a stingy person tries to find ways to make something without spending any money by using whatever irrelevant materials are redily available.

Example
Markos wanted to build a bar at home. He specified exactly how he wanted it, and then he said, 'I don't want you to spend

any money on materials because I have a lot of boxes in the garage that we can use, plus the material from the old bar.' The tradesman then gave him a dirty look, picked up his briefcase, and left. As the tradesman was on his way out, Markos said, 'Where are you going?' He replied, 'I don't do jobs like that. *Me da millo sfonjismada thhelis na gamis bittes.*'

Moral
If you don't spend money, you don't get the quality.

10. Mealon vookkon vale ma mealon lon men bis.
10. Μιάλον βούκκον βάλε, μα μιάλον λόον μεμ' πεις.
10. Take a big bite, but don't make a bad comment.

Meaning
Take a big bite, but don't make big claims.

Used
Used when one makes irresponsible comments or insinuations that can most likely be regretted later.

Example
Alexis was a racist person who one day said, 'My kids will never marry anyone from another nationality.' They all laughed at him and said, *'Mealon vookkon vale ma mealon lon men bis',* because these things happen, regardless of what the parents think. Ironically, all his children married other nationalities.

Moral
Don't make statements about things you can't control, because you don't know what the future might bring.

*11. Men **soo**zis da **bo**thkia soo brin na gavalli**je**bsis.*

11. Μεν σούζεις τα πόδκια σου πριν να καβαλλιτσέψεις.

11. Do not dangle your legs before you ride on the horse.

Angelo Ioannou and Andrew Efstathiou
Apex Park, Mildura, Australia, January 1988

Meaning

When you dangle your legs before you are ready, you risk falling off the horse.

Used

Used when one is impatient and starts something prematurely, which results in other issues.

Example

Costa was a very ambitious young man, who opened a coffee shop in the local shopping centre. He took the first week's takings and said to his father, 'I am going to buy a car.' His father then said to him, 'Why are you rushing? You still have to pay your bills out of this money. Give the business a chance to take off and make some money before you starve it. *Men soozis da bothkia soo brin na gavallijebsis.*'

Moral

Be patient and consider your priorities.

12. Men akkannis do sherin boo se daizi.
12. Μεν ακκάννεις το σιέριν που σε ταΐζει.
12. Do not bite the hand that feeds you.

Meaning
Don't bring any harm to the very people that help you. If you do, you bite the hand that feeds you.

Used
Used when one harms to the very people that helped one.

Example
Diogenis picked up a young boy who lived in the streets, gave him shelter, fed him, and decided to look after him until he found a job.

A few months later he was still unemployed and slept in every day. He was getting very aggressive and was demanding money from Diogenis all the time. One day Diogenis, as kind as he was, refused to give him money, and the young boy became very abusive. Diogenis then had had enough; kicked him out and said, '*Men akannis do sherin boo se daizi.*'

Moral
Respect the ones that helped you.

13. Me doo psilloo ppiiman.
13. Με του ψύλλου ππήδημα.
13. For a flea's leap.

Meaning
One gets in a fighting mood even over something as minute as a flea's leap.

Used
Used when one gets aggravated for the smallest reason.

Example
Jack told his mum that his new wife was acting funny lately; she was inpatient, very argumentative, and had a short fuse. She would get aggravated by the smallest thing, *'Me doo psilloo ppiiman (fleas leap).'*

His mother smiled and said, 'It's called PMS, darling, and you have to show her lots of love and understanding.'

Mum they should be calling it 'a hormone's leap', not 'a fleas leap'.

Moral
Improve your anger management skills.

(If you are married, wear a helmet and get under the bed once a month with the kids. (Joke))

14. Me don zorin o shillos en bianni laon.
14. Με το ζόριν ο σιύλλος εν πιάννει λαόν.
14. You cannot force a dog to catch a hare.

Similar to English version:
You can take the horse to the water, but you can't make it drink.

Meaning
You can take a dog hunting, but you can't make it catch a hare.

Used
Used when one is pushing another to act against his/her will.

Example
Popi was helping out a newcomer to Australia with free accommodation for a few weeks. He was too busy on his mobile all day, expecting everything from Popi.

She asked him a few times to help her with the lawnmower, but he wasn't interested. She complained to me and I said to her, 'If I was in your place, I would know what to do. I would pay him with the same currency he is paying you. Tell him to pack his bag and get out. But remember, *"Me don zorin o shillos en bianni laon."'*

Moral
It is counterproductive to push one to act unwillingly.

15. Me singenin soo fae bie je alishi verishi men kamis.
15. Με συγγενή σου φάε πιε, μα αλίσιν βερίσιν μεν κάμεις.
15. Drink and party with relatives, but
don't do business with them.

Meaning
Do not do business with relatives, as you risk spoiling the relationship.

Used
Used to advise that if you do business with relatives, you put your relationship at risk.

Example
Andrew and Nick, two brothers, decided to go into partnership and buy a supermarket. They were doing okay for a while until

they began to make money. They started arguing about money, working hours, who took more days off, and then, their wives became competitive until they came to a point where they destroyed both the partnership and their relationship.

That explains why Bappoo says, *'Me singenin soo fae bie je alishi verishi men gamis.'*

Moral
Business and relatives don't mix.

16. Medra thkio fores je gopse mian.
16. Μέτρα δκυο φορές τζαι κόψε μιαν.
16. Measure twice and cut once.

The Eureka Tower, Southbank, Melbourne

Meaning

This is a comment made by tradespeople to express the importance of double-checking measurements prior to cutting.

Used

It's used by tradespeople to stress the importance of double-checking the measurements prior to cutting.

Example
I used this proverb quite often when I was still in the furniture business, and I remember one time I took an order from a customer who lived in Melbourne's tallest building, the Eureka Tower in Southbank. It was a low-line ultra-modern hi-gloss finish entertainment unit. A few days later I was finalising the design, and I remembered that the unit had to be made in three modular pieces in order to fit in the goods elevator. I sent a tradesman to take the measurements of the elevator, and I even reminded him to double-check. Obviously, he didn't because when we delivered, the units wouldn't fit by ten centimetres. You can imagine my frustration because it wasn't something we could cut and fix; it was an 18,000-dollar unit with glass and stainless steel. We had to make a new one to keep the customer happy, and the old one I practically gave away for peanuts, incurring heavy losses.

This is where Bappoo emphasises, *'Medra thkio fores je gopse mian.'*

Moral
Double-checking is better than double-cutting.

17. Mbros gremmos je biso remma.
17. Ομπρός κρεμμός τζαι πίσω ρέμα.
17. Stuck between a cliff and a ravine.

You are cornered.

Meaning
You are caught between a cliff and a ravine.

Used
It's used when you find yourself in a predicament where you are cornered, and no matter which way you go, you can't win.

Example
Dorothy's Wedding

Dorothy was getting married, and the mother-in-law was checking out the guest list. When she saw the name Olga, one of her enemies, she was furious. 'No way,' she yelled angrily, 'It's either her or me. She is a bitch, and I don't want to see her.'

Dorothy was shocked but kept quiet. The next day she went to her mother and told her what had happened. Her mother frowned, and after a short pause, she said, 'Are you talking about Olga, my best friend?'

'Yes, Mum,' she replied. 'Over my dead body!' the mother yelled. 'If she is not in, neither am I.' Poor Dorothy was so upset, she went home crying and told her fiancé, Andros, what happened. 'What are we going to do?' she asked. *'Mbros gremmos je biso remma.'* So they both decided to keep everyone happy and send a message that it's not about the mothers and the guests but is about the couple. They decided to get married by themselves with the best man and maid of honour and then take off to Hawaii for their honeymoon.

Moral
When you are cornered, you have to jump.

N

*1. Na bier**o**si en ebi**e**rosen je yir**e**vgi je resta.*
1. Να πιερώσει εν επιέρωσεν τζαι γυρεύκει τζαι ρέστα.
1. He didn't even pay and is asking for change.

Meaning
One demanded change where one hadn't even paid.

Used
Used when one demands without entitlements or rights.

Example
Some idiot gatecrashed Tony's party and started drinking whatever he could find on the bar. He then started harassing and provoking people to fight. After a while he fell in the fish pond and ripped his shirt. Tony then lost it and kicked him out. After a few minutes he came back seeking payment for his ripped shirt. Tony asked him politely to leave at once before he called the police.

Bappoo would say, *'Na bier**o**si en ebi**e**rosen je yir**e**vgi je resta.'*

Moral
You can only demand if you have entitlements or rights.

2. Na vgi do yieman do bellon.
2. Να βκει το γαίμαν το πελλόν.
2. Let the foolish blood come out.

Christalleni, Iakovos Ioannou, and little Natasa in Ora, 1983

Meaning

Every time children get heard during play time, they lose 'foolish blood'. When all the 'foolish blood' comes out, eventually they become sensible. In other words, you need to make mistakes to learn by them and become sensible.

Used
Used when children bleed through minor injuries playing carelessly and doing crazy things that children do.

Example
The Flying Boy (True story)

I remember when I was ten years old I wanted to be an inventor. I took a cardboard box to make an aeroplane and fly from the balcony. I opened two holes, one on each end of the box, and put a rope through it. I then tied one end of the rope on the balcony and the other all the way down to the trunk of an orange tree in our front yard. I got my little brother Stelio to sit in it for a test flight, and I told him to hold on tight. Then I gave the box a push, expecting it to slide on the rope all the way down to the floor by the orange tree.

Little did I know that the rope would cut through the box shortly after 'take-off', which was exactly what happened. My poor brother was terrified and survived the crush with minor injuries – a bleeding elbow and knee. At that moment, my parents walked in and saw him on the floor crying, and I told them what happened. I was laughing hysterically because I said the aeroplane crashed, and my father chased me around the house to kill me for nearly killing my little brother. Stelios was crying not only because his knee was bleeding, but also because he was frightened. My mother took him inside and gave him first aid and said not to worry because *'Na vgi do yieman do bellon'.*

I got a good hiding from my father and was grounded for a week.

Moral
Learn from your mistakes.

3. Nisdiji i argootha en horevgi.
3. Νηστιτσή η αρκούδα εν χορεύκει.
3. A hungry bear doesn't dance.

Meaning
Priority is to get paid, not dancing.

Used
Used when one is asked to do something on an empty stomach or wallet.

Example
A mercenary went to an African country to spread a religion. After three months he sent a letter to the archbishop notifying him that he found it very difficult to get the natives' attention. 'The poor people are so hungry that they are not interested in any religion.' The archbishop then replied, 'Ah ha! Give them a hamburger each and then talk to them about anything. *Nisdidgi i argoutha en horevki.*' The rest is history.

Moral
Pay one to get action.

*1. O bath**o**s en o yiadr**o**s.*
1. Ο παθός εν ο γιατρός.
1. The sufferer is the doctor.

Meaning
When one suffers or goes through health problems, one gets to learn a lot about it and is in a position to help others with a similar condition.

Used
Used as an acknowledgement of experience of former or current sufferers, and also as an encouragement to share that experience with other sufferers of same condition.

Example
Polymyalgia Rheumatica (True story)

My close friend Teresa was diagnosed with polymyalgia rheumatica five years ago (2010). It's a condition that affects the autoimmune system. Her rheumatologist prescribed a low dosage of cortisone, but being an anti-chemical drug person, she didn't like the idea. The doctor then gave her a week to think about it.

She was devastated to find that in one week she couldn't lift her arms up and was unable to move without her husband's help; He actually had to dress her. The following day she went back to the rheumatologist and told her what had happened. She then told Teresa that in another week, if she didn't take the cortisone, she would end up in a wheelchair. She was shocked, but after thinking about it, she had no other choice but to take it.

Teresa had no idea what polymyalgia rheumatica was. She learnt about it through the Internet and a support group called the Young Women Arthritis Support Group based in the eastern suburbs of Melbourne and through a seminar organised by the Arthritis Foundation in Melbourne. She also met a professor who was one of the speakers and is now her rheumatologist.

The support group have been fantastic and have shed a lot of light on it. The exchange of experiences has been most helpful. It has helped ease the pain, as there is no cure for this condition. Teresa is a great believer of natural remedies and so were most of the members of the support group, mainly women. Their task was to share as much information as they could and, with the help of their respective rheumatologists, to develop a pain-management scheme.

Teresa is now working with a nutritionist and her rheumatologist, trying to gradually replace the chemical medicines with natural remedies, as far as they possibly can.

Sometimes, we have to accept certain conditions in our life, adapt to them, and be positive. I know it's easier said than done when you have chronic pain, but after talking to so many experts trying to find a way to help Teresa, I learnt that always there is a psychological pain with any other physical pain, like 'Why me? Why can't I dance? Why can't I do this or that? Why can't I lead a normal life?' We become negative and emotional, and go down, down, and down, stressing, looking for someone to understand our pain and realise that it's not easy. We see the pain as sharks and we are swimming between them, unable to do anything apart from keeping on swimming and hoping for the best. All this stress, of course, has such a negative effect on our immune system that it doesn't allow the system to function properly and to fight the pain.

Escape – Improve Your Quality of Life

The only choice we have is to give our immune system a boost to help us control the pain. There is no doubt that when we are happy it works better. So how do we achieve that? First of all, we have to make the big decision to accept that the diagnosis is here to stay.

Then we take a deep breath and 'take a look' at our chronic pain and say, 'You fr—n pain, I will not let you control my life. I will do anything to find ways to ignore you and free myself to live my life to the fullest.'

When you come to this point and realise what the power of mind can do, you are halfway there.

With a strong willpower and a happy immune system you can achieve miracles.

Teresa now goes to work four days a week, teaching the senior citizens crafts and other activities.

Moral
It is more beneficial to be happy with pain than to be unhappy with pain.

***2. O**bos sdrosis etsi en'na jimithis.*
2. Όπως στρώσεις έτσι εν'να τζοιμηθείς.
2. You sleep the way you make your bed.

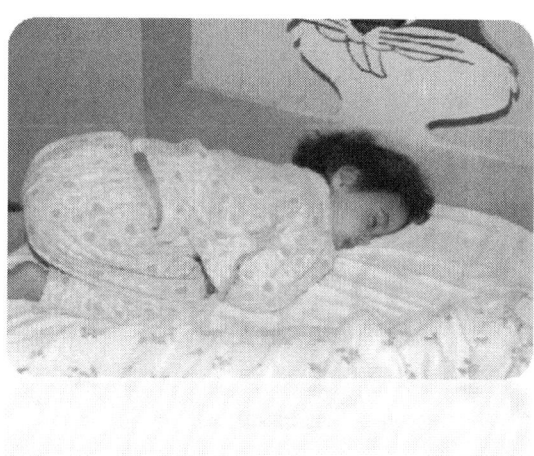

Meaning
You will sleep exactly the way you make your bed.

Used
Used as a reminder that in life you have to accept the consequences of your actions.

Example
Con is a young twenty-eight-year-old man, who is lazy, doesn't like responsibility, doesn't work, and lives on the dole, wherever he finds accommodation. He went to his uncle to borrow some money for cigarettes.

His uncle said to him, 'Why should I give you money? For the last ten years, you lived this kind of life because you have chosen to.

If you are happy, keep blaming others and continue with it. If you are not happy, do something about it to improve your life. If you place wool on your bed, you sleep warmly and comfortably. If you lie on rocks, you will sleep uncomfortably. ***O**bos sdr**o**sis **e**tsi en na jimith**is**.'*

Moral
Take full control of your life.

3. O foornos doo Hojia.
3. Ο φούρνος του Χότζια.
3. The wood-fired oven of Hodjia.

Meaning

It's a story about the wood-fired oven of Hodjia (read story below).

Used

Used when one tries to make everybody happy but oneself.

Example

The Wood-Fired Oven of Hodjia

It's a story of Hodjia, who was not a very bright person. One day, he decided to build a wood-fired oven to bake bread. He cleaned up an area in his backyard and built the oven. His wife was very happy about it, but when their neighbour came to see it, he said that it shouldn't be facing the house because the smoke will go into the house. On hearing this, Hodjia was upset, but he demolished it and built it facing away from the house.

Then another friend came over and told him that the oven should have been facing north, so he demolished it again and built it facing north.

Yet another friend came to see it, only to say that it should have been facing south. This time Hodjia scratched his head and thought for a minute. He then went and bought a wagon with four wheels and built the oven on it so he wouldn't have to demolish it again. All he had to do was to turn the wagon around to make everyone happy.

Moral
You can't please everybody, but you can please yourself.

Note
If you need to do something and you don't know how, seek advice from an expert prior to doing it. No matter what you do, people will still complain, so concentrate on what's best for you and your family.

4. O yaros o gondris ama thi do sdradoorin voora.
4. Ο γάρος ο κόντρης άμα δει το στρατούρι βουρά.
4. A donkey with ulcer on his back runs away when it sees the saddle.

English equivalent: He has a chip on his shoulder.

Meaning
The donkey had ulcer on his back and ran away at the sight of the saddle.

Used
Used when one has a guilt for a wrongdoing and another exposes one.

Example
Nesti was always bad-mouthing everybody and everything. His own son ended up in jail for many reasons, and that shut him up a bit. Every time he was at the pub and the subject of criminals came up, or there was something on TV about crime and jail, he would get up and disappear very quickly. Everybody then laughed and said, '*O yaros o gondris ama thi do sdradoorin voora.*'

Moral
If you do the wrong thing, it will come back and haunt you.

5. O aloobos ehonnedoon J'o nooros do idan bokso.
5. Ο αλουπός εχώννετουν τζ' ο νούρος του ήταν πόξω.
5. The fox was hiding, and his tail was seen.

Meaning
Like the fox that was hiding, but his big, fluffy tail was out and everyone could see it, one is trying to hide the obvious.

Used
Used to mock people for trying to hide something so obvious that it's impossible to hide it.

Example
Tim had a bald patch on top of his head, and he had a complex about it. He wanted to hide it. So he gathered all his other hair, and with the help of a tin of hair lacquer, he stuck it all on top to cover the patch and he was happy. The problem was that every time there was a bit of breeze coming through the door, the hair would lift up like a flap. Some of his mates would tease him, saying, 'Your bonnet is opened.' Bappoo would say, *'O aloobos ehonnedoon Je o nooros do idan bokso.'*

Moral
There are some things that can't be hidden.

6. *O Thheos ayaba je don gleftin, ayaba je don nigojirin.*
6. Ο Θεός αγαπά τζαι τον κλέφτην,
αγαπά τζαι τον νοικοτζύρην.
6. God loves the thief but also loves the housekeeper.

Meaning
Even though God loves the thief, God also loves the housekeeper.

Used
Used when one does, or attempts to do, the wrong thing by another and something unforeseen happens that turns things against one.

Example
Andreas attempted to unfairly, and under false pretences, take a property from his brother Sam. By coincidence, a friend of Sam's went to the titles office for an enquiry, saw Andreas there, and from his reaction realised that something was going on.

Of course, he told Sam, and after a quick investigation it was revealed that that was the case. The police were called, Andreas was charged for fraud, and Sam said, *'O Thheos ayaba je don gleftin, ayaba je don nigojirin.'*

Moral
If you do the wrong thing, you will eventually get caught.

*7. **O**son mis**o** da g**a**rdama sta yenia moo vlasd**oo**sin.*
7. Οσο μισώ τα κάρταμα στα γένια μου βλαστούσιν.
7. The more I hate cress, the more they grow on my face.

Meaning
The more I hate something, the more it seems to be happening to me.

Used
Used when something you really hate seems to be happening to you all the time.

Example
I hate chicken breasts. Every time I go to Kentucky Fried Chicken, I hope not to get breasts in my box, but you guessed it; that's exactly what I get. This shows that *'**o**son mis**o** da g**a**rdama sta yenia moo vlasd**oo**sin'.*

Moral
Need to be positive.

***8.** Odi dreksi as gadevasi.*
8. Ότι τρέξει ας κατεβάσει.
8. Whatever run will run.

Meaning
Whatever the outcome might be.

Used
Used when one doesn't care what the outcome might be.

Example
I asked the secretary of our club if he sent an application to the Multicultural Commission for a grant to buy some equipment for the seniors. He said that he didn't think that we had a chance. I suggested to send it anyway and *'**O**di dreksi as gadev**a**si'*.

Moral
Take a chance when you have nothing to lose.

9. O galos o filos odan don hriazese fenede.
9. Ο καλός ο φίλος όταν τον χρειάζεσαι φαίνεται.
9. A friend in need is a friend indeed.

Meaning
Good friends are the ones who make time for you when you need them.

Used
It is used to express disapointment to those that didn't help you when in need, or to show gratidute to those that did.

Example
Thanasis had a health scare the other day and was taken to the hospital for a check-up. His neighbour called his friend Jimmy and told him that the ambulance was there, but he wasn't sure what happened.

Jimmy dropped everything and ran to the nearest hospital to find him.

The receptionist told him, 'Yes, he is here. He is in the emergency ward, having some tests.'

Jimmy got there just in time because they needed an interpreter, as Thanasis couldn't communicate with his broken English. Thanasis's wife was worried, and Jimmy tried to comfort her as much as he could.

He waited there for five hours until they completed all the tests and the doctor told them that it was nothing serious and they could go home. Jimmy gave them a lift home and made sure that everything was okay.

Thanasis thanked him and said, *'O galos o filos odan don hriazese fenede.* Thanks for being a good friend.'

Moral
Take notice of the friends that stood by you when you needed them.

10. O galos o gabedanios sdin foordoonan fenede.
10. Ο καλός ο καπετάνιος στη φουρτούνα φαίνεται.
10. A good skipper shows in rough seas.

Meaning
You can show in bad times how good a skipper you are.

Used
Used when one has the opportunity to show action not only bruging.

Example
Jim owned a Greek restaurant in Melbourne, and he would accommodate up to 300 people, particularly on weekends.

One Saturday night I was there with my friend Christaki and his family for his wife's birthday. I was watching Jim, how he was operating in a caring manner to make everybody feel welcome, rearranging tables to accommodate larger groups; he was running up and down, trying to squeeze between tables. It was a madhouse in there, but Jim always had a smile on his face.

I asked him, 'How do you do it when you are so busy?

Christaki then said, *'O galos o gabedanios sdin foordoonan fenede.'*

Moral
The best way to judge one's ability is in worst senarios.

11. O galos o drobos vcalli je din goofin boo din driban dis.
11. Ο καλός ο τρόπος φκάλλει τζαι την
κουφήν που την τρύπαν της.
11. Kindness can make even a snake friendly.

Meaning
Even snakes are friendly when you talk to them kindly.

Used
Used as an advice to one with aggressive and offensive behaviour.

Example
A young man went to the unemployment office to register. The girl at the desk took his details and asked him to take a seat and wait for his turn as there were quite a few people before him. He wasn't happy about waiting and told the girl that he didn't have all day. The girl politely asked him why he was in such a hurry if he was unemployed. He then said to her to mind her own f—n business and became very abusive.

They then called the security and threw him out. He called his brother, who was an accountant up the road from there, and he came down.

When he told him what happened, his brother said to him that he was acting like a bloody idiot and that he had to go back and apologise, follow the rules, and be patient.

He nodded in agreement, and they both went in.

He apologised and said that he was upset because he had lost his job and assured them that it wouldn't happen again.

They both took a seat, and in 10 minutes, they were called in. After they finished, on the way out, his brother said, *'O galos o drobos vcalli je din goofin boo din driban dis.'*

Moral
Good manners make friends.

12. Ο κάττος τζ' αν εγέρασεν τα νύσια πούσιεν έσιει.
12. O kattos jan eyerasen da nishia boo'shen eshi.
12. The old cat still has his old claws.

Meaning
Like the cat that doesn't change its claws, old people don't change their bad habits.

Used
Used when old people show signs that they still have their old bad habbits.

Example
Joyce was employed by a senior citizens' hostel and worked in the kitchen. One day while she was serving the oldies their

lunches, as she passed an eighty-five-year-old man, he pinched her bottom.

She told him to keep his hands to himself, and his wife said, '*O kattos jan eyerasen da nishia boo ishen eshi.*'

Moral
It is almost impossible to change the habits of an old person.

13. Ο κόσμος τώσιει τούμπανο τζ' εμείς κρυφό καμάριν.
13. O c**o**smos d**'o**shi d**oo**mbanon j'em**is** grif**on** gama**ri**n.
13. Our precious secret that everybody knows.

Meaning
A family in the village were trying to keep a secret that everybody knew about.

Used
Used when one attempts to hide a secret that is already known to all.

Example
Vince was seen down at the creek with Tom's wife Chloe, kissing. In the next few days the whole village knew about it, but Vince and Chloe thought their secret was safe. The man at the cafe said, *'O cosmos doshi doombanon jemis grifon gamarin.'*

Moral
The walls have ears.

14. *O **noo**ros **doo** shilloo en ish**i**onni.*
14. Ο νούρος του σιύλλου εν ισιώννει.
14. You can't straighten up a dog's tail.

Meaning
Someone wanted to straighten up the tail of their dog. He cut a tube out of a cane andpushed the dog's tail into it, and after forty days, he took it out. Much to his surprise he saw that the tail curled back to its original shape.

Like the dog's tail that doesn't change, that's how some people don't change either.

Used
Used when one with certain habits and reputation promises to change but never does.

Example
The Antique Shop (True story)

My wife and I and our young friend Rafael were driving to Phillip Island from Melbourne to spend the long weekend with our friends Con and Ula.

My wife is one of those crazy antique collectors that are addicted to antique shops. As we drove down hill twards San Remo, Irene saw one of those shops and quickly said, 'Jimmy, Jimmy, take me to the antique shop.' I said, 'No way. I will never take you to an antique shop.'

She said, 'But why?'

I replied, 'I don't think I can get much for you, dear,' and we all burst out laughing. Thank God she has a sense of humour, but then I said to her that she was worth a hell of a lot more money than what they woul offer at an attique shop.

Bappoo then said, *'O n**oo**r**o**s d**oo** shill**o**o en ishi**o**nni.'*

Moral
You can't change one's character.

*15. O bell**os** boo din b**or**dan.*
15. Ο πελλός που την πόρταν.
15. The foolish with the door.

Meaning
It's about a foolish person who was told to 'bring the door with him', meaning 'to close it', and he actually pulled it out of its hinges and took it with him.

Used
Used when one misunderstands metaphors and creates funny scenes with one's actions.

Example
Zavos was told to bring the goat to drink water, and he carried it on his shoulders. They laughed and said you are like *'O bell**os** boo din b**or**dan'*.

Moral
Deal with sensible people.

*16. **O**boo **e**shi gabn**o**n **e**shi je fothki**a**n.*
16. Οπου έσιει καπνόν έσιει τζαι φωδκιάν.
16. Where there is smoke, there is fire.

Meaning
Where there is smoke, there must be fire.

Used:
Used when something is obvious, and you don't need proof.

Example
Trevor was the despatch manager of a timber wholesaler. The boss was looking for the invoice of a customer that had called earlier on enquiring about a delivery, and he couldn't find it. When he asked Trevor, he said to leave it to him. The boss was concerned and secretly kept an eye on things only to see that Trevor made cash sales with no invoice. He wanted to set up surveillance cameras to catch him, and his wife said, *'**O**boo **e**shi gabn**o**n **e**shi je fothki**a**n.'*

Moral
There is no need to see the fire if you see the smoke.

17 O fovos ferni golasin.
17. Ο φοος φερνει κολασην.
17. Fear brings hell.

Meaning
When you are fearful of hell, you do the right thing.

Used
Used when one gives up an offence after something scares the hell out of one.

Example
Who Smashes the Windows? (True story)

My friend Dimitri had a warehouse with offices in Kensington, an inner suburb of Melbourne. There were a few large glass windows in the front, which allowed the sun to go through and brighten up the place. Dimitri had a problem with the kids in the area as they were quite rough. The building was near a school, and obviously there were many children around. The shop was closed during the weekend, and some of the children were doing silly things like graffiti or smashing windows and even the public telephone boxes on the corner.

Dimitri would call the police at least every second Monday to report it.

The police would take a statement and give Dimitri a copy to claim from his insurance. This continued on for a few years. The insurance company made him fit protective grills, extra lights, cameras, you name it. It cost him a fortune, but the biggest problem was that the insurance company refused to insure him any more unless he paid an astronomical amount of money, which he didn't have.

He was in a dilemma and didn't know what to do. He rang the police sergeant to come for coffee and try to find a solution. When the sergeant came in, Dimitri told him his predicament and also how disappointed he was with the police for not providing him protection.

The sergeant then asked what he intended to do, and Dimitri replied, 'It's very simple. I will protect my own property since you can't do it. I will sleep in here if I have to and call the police when I see them.'

The sergeant got up, and before he walked out, he said, 'I hope you don't do anything stupid. You can't take the law into your own hands.'

An hour later Dimitri saw a little kid, with a familiar face, walking into the milk bar across the road. He went up to him as he came out of the shop and said, 'I know that you know who smashes my windows every couple of weeks. If you tell me who it is, I'll buy you an ice cream.'

The kid's eyes popped out, and he said, 'It is Darren the teacher's son,' and pointed at the fourth house from the corner. Dimitri then bought him an ice cream and walked up to the teacher's house. He knocked at the door where a blonde lady answered. Dimitri introduced himself and told her what the problem was and that he believed her son Darren was responsible.

On hearing this she went crazy and started yelling in an offensive manner, denying that her son had any involvement. He then very calmly said, 'Okay, I am sorry to have disturbed you, but just before I go I'd like to inform you that as of tonight I will be sleeping in there to catch the offender. I am glad that your son is not involved, so you have nothing to worry about.'

By the time Dimitri walked back to his office, three police cars surrounded the building with the sirens on and guns. They put him against the wall and asked him where the gun was. He frowned and said, 'What gun?'

The blonde lady then came yelling again, 'That's him! That's him.'

The sergeant then said, 'We had a report from this lady that you want to kill her son with a shotgun.'

Dimitri then said, 'I don't have a gun. I just told her that I will sleep the night in here to catch the offender.'

'Yes, yes,' she said. 'That's exactly what he said, you see?'

When the sergeant realised what had happened and that there was no gun involved, he told her to keep quiet and go home before he charged her for misleading the police. Later on that night, at about six o'clock, Dimitri came back to the shop with his wife, who dropped him off and left. He took his time walking in and made sure all the kids outside the milk bar saw him. The word went around very fast that Dimitri will be in there to catch the offender.

Little did they know that he jumped out through the back window where his wife was waiting for him to take him home.

Ever since that incident and for the remaining ten months of his lease, there was not one breakage, and the telephone boxes on the corner were unattackec as well. That's when Bappoo says, 'When you are fearful of hell you do the right thing.'

Moral
A slap on the wrist now can prevent jail later.

18. Obios jinia thkio laoos, hanni doos je doos thkio.
18. Οποιος τζυνηά δκιο λαούς, χάννει τους τζαι τους δκιο.
18. Who hunts two hares at the same time loses them both.

Meaning
When you are greedy and try to do two things in at the same time, you lose them both. Just like when you chase two rabbits at the same time.

Used
Used when one rushes to do two things at the same time.

Example
A taxi driver at the airport was being greedy and trying to get two customers at the same time. They were not happy about it, and they jumped into other taxis and were gone before he could blink.

Another taxi driver was watching and said to him, **'O***bios jinia thkio la**oo**s, h**a**nni doos je doos thki**o**.'*

Moral
You have a better chance of succeeding if you concentrate on one thing at a time.

*19. O bell**o**s ebojim**i**thhin, je bell**o**n **o**roman **i**then.*
19. Ο πελλός εποτσοιμήθην τζαι πελλόν οροµαν είδεν.
19. The foolish had a foolish dream.

Meaning

Foolish people usually have foolish desires that they dream about.

Used

Used when one shares a foolish dream with friends.

Example

Hodjia's Lotto Dream

Nastradin Hojia woke up at three o'clock in the morning and sat up in his bed, quite disturbed and sweating. His wife woke up and asked him if he was okay. He replied, 'You wouldn't believe what happened. I had a dream that I won a million dollars in the lotto!' His wife said to him, 'You idiot, why didn't you put the money in the bank before you woke up?'

Bappoo then said, *'O bell**o**s ebojim**i**thhin, je bell**o**n **o**roman **i**then.'*

Moral

Be realistic.

20. O pseftis je o gleftis don brodon hronon sheroonde.
20. Ο ψεύτης τζαι ο κλέφτης τον πρώτον χρόνον σιαίρουνται.
20. Liars and thieves are happy only the first year.

> You can fool some people sometimes,
> but not all people all the time.

Meaning
Those who steal lie or do the wrong thing by others will only be happy temporarily.

Used
Used when one is caught doing illegal or immoral activities.

Example
Harry used to import olive oil in 200-litre drums from Greece, re-bottle it in smaller containers, and sell it direct to public. His oil was good quality, and there was quite a big demand for it. After a year he got greedy and started cheating by mixing it with low-quality vegetable oil. That was a bad decision because Europeans know their oils, and when they realised that he cheated, it was the end of his business. Bappoo then said, *'O pseftis je o gleftis don brodon hronon sheroonde.'*

Moral
You can only fool some people some of the times.

***21.** **O**bios annii don **l**akkon doo **a**lloo p**e**fti o **i**thios m**e**sa.*
21. Οποιος αννοίει τον λάκκον του
άλλου, ππέφτει ο ίδιος μέσα.
21. Who open's someone else's grave falls in it himself.

Meaning
If you dig someone's grave you fall in it yourself.

Used
Used when a wicked person attempts to do harm to someone, and it backfires.

Example
Kakos went to burn a house for revenge. He accidentally spilt petrol on himself, and when he lit the fire he got badly burned. Bappoo then said, *'**O**bios annii don **l**akkon doo **a**lloo p**e**fti o **i**thios m**e**sa.'*

Moral
What goes around comes around.

22. Obios anacad**o**nnete me da b**i**dera dr**o**ndon i **o**rnithhes.
22. Οποιος ανακατώννεται με τα πίτερα τρων' τον οι όρνιθες.
22. If you mix with the chicken food, you get eaten by chickens.

Meaning
Getting involved in other people's problems can get you in trouble:

Used
Used as a warning that when one interferes in other people's problems, one is looking for trouble.

Example
Tom's next-door neighbour was abusing his wife badly, and the whole neighbourhood heard the commotion. Tom then called the police, but they let him off with a warning that next time he will be arrested. The following morning Tom found all the tyres of his car flat and ripped. Tom's wife then said, '**O**bios anacad**o**nnete me da b**i**dera dr**o**ndon i **o**rnithhes.'

Moral
It is wise to mind your own business.

***23. O**bios th**e**li da bol**la** hanni je da llia.*
23. Οποιος θέλει τα πολλά, χάννει τζαι τα λλία.
23. Who wants the lot loses even the few.

Meaning
When you are greedy and want everything, you lose the lot.

Used
Used as a warning to greedy people that want to grab everything.

Example
Alex was offered one million dollars to sell his building. That was double what the actual value was, but the buyer was planning to build a shopping complex in the area and Alex's property was the last of the ten that they needed to acquire. When Alex realised that they needed it no matter what, he asked for two million dollars, not-negotiable. After several attempts to negotiate failed, the company changed their plans and withdrew the offer, moving to the next block. Now Alex's property is worth no more than half a million. He lost half a million dollars because of his greediness. Bappoo said, **'O**bios th**e**li da bol**la** hanni je da llia.'

Moral
Don't be greedy.

24. *O g*olos *o ditsiros ithen do vrajin je eshestin.*
24. Ο κώλος ο τίτισρος είδεν το βρατσίν τσ' εσιέστην.
24. The naked buttock saw underpants and shat itself.

Meaning
When you put underpants on a poor man's bottom for the first time, he shits himself from joy.

Metaphorically, it means poor villagers become rich and act as if they are aristocrats.

Used
It's used to express one's disgust when neo-rich people look down at others.

Example
The Success of Mr Drahanas

Mr and Mrs Drahanas migrated to Australia from a remote village on one of the Greek islands, looking for a better future for their three little kids. They had a problem with their English, but somehow Mr Drahanas managed to get a job at Massey Fergusson Tractors and Machinery.

Mrs Drahanas was the housekeeper and also managed all their finances. She must have been pretty good at it because after a couple of years, and with the help of some friends, they bought restaurant equipment and set up a fish and chips shop. They had no education, but still with broken English, lots of guts, and hard work, they managed to do well and to eventually buy the building.

Not long after, the area was re-zoned by the council from industrial to residential, which increased its value by 300%.

Before they finished the celebrations, they received a letter from a large corporation that they were planning to knock all the buildings down and build a sixty-storey skyscraper.

Mr Drahanas's shop was in a prime corner position, and they offered him an astronomical amount to sell. Eventually he did, and with the money he bought a double-storied house in Toorak, a Mercedes for himself, and a BMW for his wife, and he enrolled his kids in a private school.

The balance of the money he invested in apartments, and he is now very well off. He and his wife worked very hard and they are to be congratulated, but there is one thing about them that I resent. They look down on people and don't want to mix with 'low-class' people. All of a sudden they are 'members of the royal family'. The idea of being rich has gone to their head, and this is a case where Bappoo says, *'O golos o ditsiros ithen doe vrajin je eshestin.'*

Moral
Don't forget your roots, and treat all as equals.

25. *O yaros mian foran goodoolla sto thendron je boirizi.*
25. Ο γάρος μια φορά κουτουλλά στο δέντρον τζαιποϋρίζει.
25. A donkey hit's a tree once, never goes past it again.

Meaning
Even a donkey learns by its mistakes.

Used
Used when one doesn't learn by one's mistakes and keeps repeating them.

Example
Paul is a kind cabinet-maker, and he deals with a couple of builders that give him a hard time and don't want to pay on time. They always stretch the payment and complain that he is very expensive, and even when they pay the bill they still dock the bill and take all his profit.

He complained to me the other day that he quoted them for a big job, gave them near-cost price, and they were still complaining. I said to him, 'They treat you like an idiot. What's the point of doing the work if you don't make any profit? You lost money with them so many times, why you are still supplying them?' Bappoo then said, '*O yaros mian foran goodoolla sto thendron je boirizi.*'

Moral
Learn by your mistakes.

26. O yaros o ogniaris, en je vari yomarkaris.
26. Ο γάρος ο οκνιάρης εν τζαι βαρυγομαρκάρης.
26. The lazy donkey overloads himself.

Meaning
When one is lazy, one carries more than one can handle to finish quickly.

Used
It's used to discourage the lazy from overloading themselves.

Example
Nicholas was working on a building site, and the boss told him to carry only five bricks at a time, but because he was lazy to do more trips, he carried ten, taking a risk to damage his back. His boss then said, *'O yaros o ogniaris, en je vari yomarkaris.'*

Moral
Don't carry more than what you can handle.

*27. **O**la d'**a**shen i Mario**ri**, o fere**jes** tis **e**libe.*
27. Ολα τάσιεν η Μαριορή, ο φερετσές της έλειπε.
27. With Marjory's health problems, the last
thing on her mind should be the barque.

Meaning
With all Marjory's health problems the last thing she should be interested in would be the burqa.

Used
Used when one has serious issues and worries about trivial things.

Example
Young Harry was pulled over by the police for speeding and going through red lights on the way from the airport to Larnaca. They asked him for his licence, but he didn't have one, as he'd already lost it for other offences. They then conducted a breathalysing test which showed a reading of twice the legal limit. The policeman asked him to step out of the car and put his hands on the bonnet. After a quick search they found a big bag of cannabis in the car. Of course, they arrested him and put him in custody, charged with various offences. The police called his father to come and pick up his car. Harry then said, 'Tell my dad to wash my car when he takes it home.' Bappoo then said, *'**O**la d'**a**he i Mario**ri**, o fere**jes** tis **e**libe.'*

Moral
Get your priorities right.

Management Test (Answers from page 95)

The correct answer is

1. Important
2. Urgent
3. Need to do
4. Like to do.

Doing the important things today minimises the urgent things tomorrow.

***28.** Osa ban je osa'rtoon.*
28. Οσα παν τζ' όσα έρτουν.
28. Whatever goes, whatever comes.

Meaning
There is no control and whatever happens.

One doesn't manage one's finances properly and spends money irresponsibly and wastefully.

Used
Used when one is wasteful and displays poor money management skills.

Example
The Tea Tin

I remember when I was about ten years old I asked Grandfather Thimidros to give me ten cents that I needed for my school excursion, and said I would pay him back the following week. He pointed at a tea tin sitting on the shelf and said, 'There are some coins in that tin. Have a look if there are enough.' I did and found 11 cents, of which I took 10.

I thanked him and left. Three weeks later I went to my grandpa again to ask for another loan of 10 cents for something else. He pointed at the same tea tin on the shelf. Happy as a lark, I climbed on the chair and reached for it, only to find that there was only one cent in it. I turned to him very disappointedly and said, 'Grandpa, there is only one cent in the tin!'

He then replied, smiling, 'Ah ha! Have you put the money you owe back in the tin?'

I said, 'No.'

He then said, 'Come here and sit on my lap.'

I did so and he said, 'Listen here very carefully. What I am about to tell you you must remember forever and you will never run out of money. If you always pay your debts first, you will always have money to pay your debts. *If you want to accumulate money in that tin, you have to put in more than what you take out.* This is the basic principle of good money management. If it's the other way around, you will always be broke.'

Then Bappoo says, **'*Osa ban je osa ertoon.*'**

Moral
Never spend more than what you earn.

29. O shillos boo lassi, en akkanni.
29. Ο σιύλλος που λάσσει εν ακκάννει.
29. Dogs that bark don't bite.

Meaning
A dog that barks usually doesn't bite. A person that makes a lot of noise, yells, swears, threatens, etc. in actual fact is harmless.

Used
Used when one talks loud and makes a lot of noise trying to scare or impress others.

Example
A few young lads surrounded an old man in a dark alley, yelling at him, trying to scare him into handing his money over.

The old man very confidently took a karate stance and said, 'Okay, who is going to hit me first?' In two minutes flat they disappeared. A lady passing by said to him that was very quick.

The old man replied, *'O shillos boo lassi, en akkanni.'*

Moral
Talkers usually are not doers.

30. O shillos ji boo droi, ji lassi.
30. Ο σιύλλος τζει που τρώει τζει λάσσει.
30. The dog barks where he eats.

Meaning
Dogs are so loyal to their owners that will do anything to protect them.

Used
Used when one doesn't show the required loyalty to the people that look after one.

Example
Kostas lives with his uncle, while he is studying at the university. They don't charge him board, but they expect him sometimes to help with the housework. He doesn't lift a finger to do any work at home, but he helps the neighbour to mow his lawn every now and again. One day his uncle came home as he

was doing it and gave him a dirty look. He was very upset, but he didn't say anything. Bappoo then said, *'O shillos ji boo droi, ji lassi.'*

Moral
Be loyal to the ones that care for you.

31. *O*bios viazete scond*a*fti.
31. Οποιος βιάζεται σκοντάφτει.
31. Who rushes trips.

Meaning
Who is in hurry runs the risk of having an accident.

Used
Used when one makes costly mistakes because one rushes.

Example
Andrew is a very impatient person. He drives a forklift to load trucks. He is always in a hurry and causes a lot of damage.

One day when I was there, he picked up a whole pack of timber from the top shelf; rushed to finish quickly, he reversed very fast and smashed into a trailer. He then hit the brakes, and the pack went flying on to the truck, causing a lot of damage. They were very lucky that no one was hurt.

I said to him, 'What's the point of rushing? *O*bios viazete scond*a*fti?'

Moral
Work carefully.

***32.** Obios en thheli na zimosi bende meres goshinizi.*
32. Οποιος εν θέλει να ζυμώσει πέντε μέρες κοσιηνίζει.
32. Who doesn't want to bake sifts for five days.

Meaning
When one doesn't want to bake, one drags sifting on and on.

Used
Used when one procrastinates and keeps postponing things.

Example
My wife accidentally broke the handle of one of her china cup collection. She asked me if I could fix it with superglue, and I said, 'Okay, leave it on my desk.' She was quite anxious to have it fixed, and she kept on coming back for three days. On the

fourth day she came in, and if looks could kill I would be dead by now. She then said, '***O**bios en thheli na zim**o**si bende meres goshin**i**zi.'*

Moral
Where there is no will nothing happens.

33. O voscos o pseftis.
33. Ο βοσκός ο ψεύτης.
33. The lying shepherd.

English equivalent: Crying wolf.

Meaning
The shepherd boy raised a false alarm, and people lost trust in him.

Used
Used when one has a habit of lying.

Example
Aesop's Fable

A shepherd boy played jokes with the villagers, calling, 'A wolf is attacking my sheep!' When the villagers rushed to help, he laughed at them. He did it a second time, and again he laughed at them. The villagers were not happy with that at all. A few days later, wolves really attacked his sheep, but when he called for help, none of the villagers turned up to help, simply because they didn't believe him. He had got a bad reputation that he was a liar. The wolves destroyed his sheep, and no one helped him.

Bappoo then said, '*O voscos o pseftis.*'

Moral
If you want people to trust you, don't lie.

> **34. Oolli lesin je bolen, je o ftohos ji boo boni.**
> 34. Ούλλοι λέσιν τζαι πολέν τζ' ο φτωχός τζει που πονεί.
> 34. Everybody about the issue, and the poor about his pain.

Meaning
While everyone in the village was talking about a common problem, the poor man only complained about his empty stomach.

Used
Used when one's main concern is one's own problem and doesn't care about other issues.

Example
The local Member of Parliament went to the village to discuss the issue of the freeway bypassing the village. The residents were concerned that it would destroy the village's business.

Everyone expressed their concerns but Stamatis. He kept on saying, 'My stomach is empty. My stomach is empty.' That was his only concern.

The mayor then said, **'Oolli lesin je bolen, je o ftohos ji boo boni.'**

Moral
Everyone knows one's own problem.

*35. **Oo**lli yia din mana mas rod**oo**n.*
35. Ούλλοι για την μάνα μας ρωτουν.
35. All for our mother are interested.

Meaning
All the men are interested in our mother because she is beautiful; nobody is interested in our father.

Used
Used when others discover that you have something of interest to them and they suddenly become friendly.

Example
Used when politicians show interest in you and send you 'love letters' prior to election time. Bappoo then says, **'Oo***lli yia din mana mas rod**oo**n.*'

Moral
Sudden interest from others should raise questions.

*36. **O**boo ibarhi thelisi, ibarhi je o drobos.*
36. Οπου υπάρχει θέλειση, υπάρχει τζαι ο τρόπος.
36. Where there is a will, there is a way.

Meaning
If we really and wholeheartedly want to achieve something, we can find a way to do it.

Used
Used as an encouragement to one to find a way to do something.

Example
The Donkey That Fell Down into the Well

It's a story I saw on Facebook of a farmer's donkey that fell into a well and the owner called the villagers to help him get it out. Unfortunately, the donkey was too heavy, and despite all the attempts, it was impossible to get him out. The owner then told everybody that the donkey was too old anyway and to shovel dirt into the well to bury him so he wouldn't suffer too long in there.

They all agreed and started shovelling dirt on top of the donkey. About an hour later, when the well was almost full, a little boy yelled, 'Stop! Stop! The donkey is alive, standing on top of the dirt!' All were astonished to see the donkey on top of the dirt. The farmer then said to keep throwing dirt on top of him; he would shake it off and take a step upwards.

Bappoo said, *'**O**boo ibarhi thelisi, ibarhi je o drobos.'*

The donkey found a way to get out and said, 'Every time you come across a problem, use it as a stepping stone to get out of it.'

Moral
Shake off the dirt and take a step upwards.

P

1. Psahni yia psilloos mes dashera.
1. Ψάχνει για ψύλλους μες τ' άσιερα.
1. Looking for nits in the haystack.

Meaning
One is searching for something tiny in a place where it is almost impossible to find – like looking for needles in the haystack.

Used
Used when one has undertaken an impossible task.

Example
Tom and Con went fishing in Port Phillip Bay in a little dinghy. At one stage as Tom was casting his line, his wedding ring slipped through his fingers and went flying into the sea. He was devastated. He quickly got undressed and kept on diving in with much determination to find it.

Con said to him, 'You are wasting your time. You cannot even see the ocean floor, and you expect to find the ring? *Psahnis yia psilloos mes dashera.*'

Moral
Don't waste time and effort on impossible tasks.

S

1. Spire na ttherisis.
1. Σπύρε να θερίσεις.
1. Sow to harvest.

Meaning
If a farmer doesn't put in the work to sow, cultivate, and water the farm, he will not have a crop to harvest.

Used
Used when one expects benefits when one hasn't put in the effort.

Example
Mr Tembelhanas was a very lazy person in the village, who didn't want to work. He lived off everyone, blaming all and his luck for his condition.

One day the villagers woke up to him and refused to feed him unless he got off his bum and worked for it. They said to him, *'Spire na ttherisis.'*

Moral
You have to work to have the benefits.

2 Stoo coofoo din borda, oso thhelis vronda.
2. Στου κουφού την πόρτα όσο θέλεις βρόντα.
3. On a deaf's door knock as much as you like.

English version: Fall on deaf ears.

Meaning
A deaf doesn't hear the knock on the door, no matter how hard you knock.

Used
Used when one doesn't respond to your repeated attempts to get one's attention.

Example
Apparently my wife had asked me a few times if I had taken the rubbish bins out for collection. I was so involved with what I was doing on the computer that I didn't hear a word. Next morning I remembered only when I heard the truck picking up from the neighbours. My wife then said, 'I reminded you last night, but *stoo coofoo din borda, oso thhelis vronda.*'

Moral
Ensure you get one's attention to make a point.

My Hearing Test

I went to my friend George, who is an audiologist, to seek advice about my wife's hearing. She didn't seem to respond when I talked to her, and I was concerned. I did not know how to tell her, and George suggested that I do a simple test.

'Go home,' George said. 'When you see her, talk to her from about twenty metres away. Ask her something. If she doesn't respond, go three metres closer and repeat that every three metres until you get a response.'

I went home that afternoon. I opened the front door and saw her in the kitchen, cooking dinner. She looked at me, waved, and continued her cooking. I then asked her from where I was standing what she was cooking, but there was no reply. I took a few steps forward and repeated the same question. Again, there was no response. I tried again and again but nothing. Finally, I was three metres away and asked her, for the fifth time, what she was cooking. She then gave me such a look and yelled, 'For God's sake, I am telling you for the fifth time, spaghetti bolognaise!'

*3. St**oo**s dif**loo**s vasil**e**vi o mon**of**thhalmos.*
3. Στους τυφλούς βασιλεύει ο μονόφθαλμος.
3. In the kingdom of the blind, the one-eyed is a king.

Meaning

In a community with uneducated people the semi-educated is the king.

Used

Used when there is shortage of qualified people and we have to accept the next best.

Example

The priest was the most educated person in the village. Everyone would take their letters or documents to him to read for them, and every time he would say, 'Give me one minute to wear my reading glasses.' Mr Themis was a very ambitious man, who always wanted to become a *mouhtari* (mayor) of the village, but there was a problem; he had very little education. He was smart enough, though, to figure out how to solve the problem. He figured out that if the priest could read simply by wearing his reading glasses, then all he had to do was buy a pair of reading glasses.

He went to the optician and asked for reading glasses. He had test after test; he tried all different lenses, and he still couldn't read. The optician was puzzled and at one stage asked him if he could read. His replied, 'If I could read, why would I be looking for reading glasses?'

He became a *mouhtari* anyway, and Bappoo said, '*Stoos difloos vasilevi o monofthhalmos.*'

Moral
In the event of shortage we lower our standards.

4. Stin anerkan fela je do halazin.
4. Στην ανερκάν φελά τζαι το χαλάζι.
4. In the drought, hail is good enough.

Meaning
If there is no rain to water, the garden hail will do.

Used
Used when we have no choice but to settle with what is available.

Example
One Sunday I went mushroom-picking in the pine forest of Mt Macedon with a couple of friends. We ran around for two hours, and we were starving.

On the way back we stopped at the local service station to see if they had anything to eat. The only thing they had was some dried-out pies in the warmer. We all hated meat pies, but we were so hungry that we said, *'Stin anerkan fela je do halazin.'*

Moral
Sometimes we have to settle for what we get.

5. Sirne avka bass don dihon, golloon?
5. Σύρνε αυκά πας τον τοίχον, κολλούν;
5. Throw eggs on the wall, do they stick?

Meaning
Like whole eggs don't stick to the wall, that's how my words don't stick to your head.

Used
Used when one doesn't pay any attention to you, no matter how hard you try.

Example
I must have told the boys at work ten times to keep the sink clean in the lunch room. I put a notice on the fridge and keep reminding them, but to no avail. *'Sirne avka bass don dihon, golloon?'*

Moral
Reconsider your methods of attracting attention.

6. Shillon blinnis shillon loosis, bale shilies mirizi.
6. Σιύλλον πλύννεις, σιύλλον λούσεις, πάλαι σιυλλιές μυρίζει.
6. A dog would always smell like a dog even if you wash it.

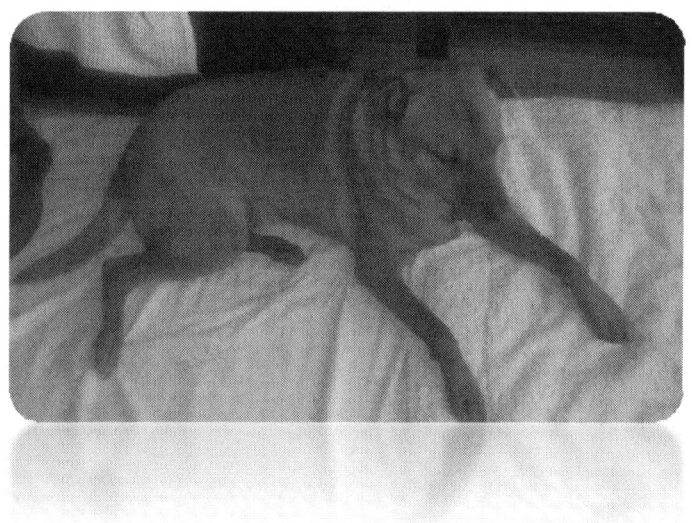

Meaning
You can't change the nature of a person, like you can't change the smell of a dog.

Used
Used as an expression when one's character doesn't change.

Example
Nikos was a compulsive gambler since he was very young. When he married Andria, he promised that he would stop gambling. Ten years and two kids later she was still struggling and tolerating him – being broke, never being home – and getting by with the help of her parents.

Her father told her to piss him off, because he was a useless bastard and would never change. *'Shillon blinnis shillon loosis, bale shilies mirizi.'*

Moral
You can't change one's character.

T

1. Thheli je do psoomin soston je don shillon hortadon.
1. Θέλει τζαι το ψουμί σωστό τζαι τον σιύλλο χορτάτον.
1. He wants the bread whole and the dog fed.

Similar to English version:
You can't have your cake and eat it too.

Meaning
You want the dog fed and the bread whole.

Used
Used when one is greedy and demands everything to be his/her way.

Example
Mr Spangos was obsessed with saving money. You couldn't get him to spend one cent unless he considered it from every aspect. Even when he bought a litre of milk for his own baby, he would ask his wife to pay him half of the money.

I wonder whether she charges him half when she breastfed the baby! Her father kept saying, 'This is ridiculous! What sort of a father or husband could he be, with two wallets in one family?' The other day, he came home and asked her what she had cooked. She said, 'Nothing. There is no shopping in the pantry.' You can't have your pay envelope full and food in the pantry. Like Bappoo said, '*Thheli je do psoomin soston je don shillon hortadon.*'

Moral
Compromise and don't be greedy.

2. Theli golajion do moron, na vali noon me don jeron.
2. Θέλει κολατσιόν το μωρό, να βάλει νουν με τον τζαιρόν.
2. Be gentle with kids; they'll mature in time.

Little Angelo Karaiskakis, 2011,
helping mummy with painting.

Meaning
Children need kindness and tenderness until they mature.

Used
Used when one is inpatient and aggressive with the children because they don't listen.

Example

Theodore and his wife Rita I have known since they were kids. They had a three-year-old boy and a five-year-old girl. They were beautiful kids. Rita stayed home looking after them, and Theodore had a delivery van doing courier service. They were a beautiful family, but Theodore had a temper that he couldn't control. Occasionally, he would come home tired and agitated and would pick on the kids for the smallest thing. He didn't have patience to talk to them nicely. He yelled at them and spoke to them with a lot of anger. Once I happened to be there to witness something that made me very unhappy. I got up to leave, and he asked me where I was going.

I said, 'I can't tolerate this kind of behaviour.' He and the kids ran up to me and said, 'Please, don't go.' I thought for a minute and then I said, 'Okay, as long as you promise me that you will do something about your anger, perhaps an anger management course.'

He looked at his wife, and she nodded her head, agreeing with me; then he looked at the kids and said, 'You are right. I am sorry. I will do something about it.' His wife then came and gave him a hug and a kiss and thanked him.

I then said, *'Theli golajion do moron, na vali noon me don jeron.'*

Moral
Be firm but gentle with children.

3. Thimos doo horkadi, zimia doo boonjioo doo.
3. Θυμός του χωρκάτη, ζημιά του πουντζού του.
3. Villager's anger, loss to his purse.

Meaning
Angry villagers usually make decisions that result in their loss.

Used
Used when an angry person makes instantaneous decisions that costs one dearly.

Example
The Man with the Jack

A man was driving his car through the mountains on a dirt road. Suddenly one of his tyres went flat. He stopped the car, opened the boot, took the spare tyre out to replace it, and much to his disappointment the jack was missing.

That infuriated him because he was running late for an appointment.

He yelled and kicked the car a few times to get his frustration out, and then he stopped and said to himself, 'Going crazy will not get me anywhere. Let's think how I am going to get out of this situation.'

He looked around him, and though it was very dark, his eye caught a light up on top of the mountain. As he was calming down, he thought, 'If there is a light up there, there should be a house. I'd better make my way up there to ask if they have a jack to lend me.'

After a few minutes' walking, Mr. Negative started whispering in his ear, 'Hey, what happens if you go all the way up there and nobody is home?'

That made him mad again, but he calmed himself and continued the walk up the mountain. Not long after that, Mr Negative came back and whispered, 'What if they are home but don't have a jack?'

That was enough to fire him up again, and he started swearing and yelling. He then sat down and calmed himself again. Taking a deep breath, he set off again.

Eventually, he arrived outside the house. But before he knocked on the door, Mr Negative came to him again and whispered, 'And what if the man is home but he is not very helpful and he doesn't want to give you his jack?'

This was the last straw. His vision became blurry and his thoughts unclear. The poor man opened the door with a smile, but before he could speak, the man jumped in and said, 'Well, you can shove your blooming jack up your backside!' Bappoo then said, *'Thimos doo horkadi, zimia doo boonjioo doo.'*

Moral
Decisions made in distress are usually wrong.

4. *Thos doo belloo loocanicon, je na soo be ma en zavon.*
4. Δως του πελλού λουκάνικον τζαι να σου πει μα εν ζαβόν.
4. Give a fool a sausage to complain that it's not straight.

Meaning
You give a sausage to a starving fool, and instead of being appreciative, he complains about the shape of it.

Used
Used when one foolishly rejects something valuable and beneficial for trivial reasons.

Example
I was invited to a friend's place for dinner once, and I witnessed something that attracted my attention. The young twenty-two-year-old daughter was so spoilt that she asked her mummy to peel the egg for her and take the pips out of the olives, or take the chicken meat off the bone for her etc. I said to her mother, 'Do you still breastfeed her?'

She replied, 'You haven't seen anything yet. Last year I deposited 10,000 euros in a bank account that I opened for her, and she yelled at me, complaining that I opened the account with the wrong bank.'

Bappoo said, '*Thos doo belloo loocanicon, je na soo be ma en zavon.*'

Moral
See the actual value of things.

*5. Thos doo tharros doo horkadi, jen'na mbi
me des boines mes'do grevadin.*
5. Δώστου θάρρος του χωρκάτη τζ' εννά
μπει με τες ποϊνες στο κρεβάτι.
5. Encourage the villager, and he will get in bed with the boots.

Similar to English version:
Give him your finger, and he will grab your hand.

Meaning
Encourage the hillbillies, and they can be inconsiderate and take advantage of you.

Used
Used when one takes advantage of your hospitality.

Example
You invite your neighbour over to use your swimming pool. Not only does he come over but he takes over the house, eats your

lunch, drinks a bottle of whisky, helps himself to everything, and wants to stay for dinner as well. That's when you say, *'Thos doo tharros doo horkadi, jen'na mbi me des boines mesdo grevadin.'*

Moral
Be cautious of the ones that take advantage of you.

My grandfather used to say, 'Be kind, but don't forget that there is a limit to kindness. When you go over the limit it becomes stupidity.'

6. *Thakk**a**nni d'**o**nan, je bon**oo**n don **oo**lla.*
6. Δακκάννει τόναν τζαι πονούν τον ούλα.
6. He bites the one (finger), and they all heard.

Meaning
The one stuffed up badly and now bites one's fingers.

Used
Used when one makes an ill-thought decision that results in a disaster.

Example
The taxation office charged Ted for tax avoidance, and he had to sell his house to pay the fine and what he owed.

Now Bappoo says, *'Thakkanni d'onan, je bonoon don oolla.'*

Moral
Consider all aspects before you make a decision.

The Boss's House (Joke)

Yong was working as a chef in a restaurant. He always tried to do the right thing and was very quiet. One Friday morning, he rang his boss and said in broken English, 'Sorry, Boss, me sick today, no feeling good.'

On hearing this, the boss exclaimed, 'Oh no, Yong, today is a very busy day, and I really need you. I am going to give you a piece of advice. I'll tell you a secret. When I feel sick in the morning I ask my wife to make me a cup of green tea with two Panadols, then have sex and another cup of tea with brandy, and in half an hour I feel perfect. I suggest you do the same.'

Yong paused for a minute and said, 'Well, we'll see.'

Two hours later, Peter showed up at work as happy as lark, hopping and whistling.

The boss looked at him happily and said, 'I am so glad you took my advice, Yong.' Yong then replied, 'Yes, Boss, it was an excellent idea. By the way, you have very nice house, Boss.'

Then Bappoo said, *'Thakkanni donan, je bonoon don oolla.'*

7. *Thame se thelo gavoora, na drappias da garvoona.*
7. Δαμέ σε θέλω κάβουρα να τραππιάς τα κάρβουνα.
7. Here you are, crab, jump out of the fire.

Meaning
The crab was bragging that even though it walks sideways, it can get out of any situation. When they put him on the red charcoals of the BBQ, it couldn't jump out.

Used
Used to challenge one that brags to show how good one is.

Example
Theo always bragged that he was the best in everything he did. One long weekend, we decided, with all the boys, to go four-wheel driving. We got our camping gear out, set up the tents, and the kids collected wood for the fire. We took two four-wheel drives, of which Theo was driving one. The ground was quite wet and slippery because of torrential rain the day before. Theo and I decided to go for a bit of exploration before it got dark. As we were driving, I could feel the car slipping sideways.

I said, 'Theo, take it easy, mate. The ground is very soft. But he deliberately skidded and yelled, 'Youuuuhouuuu! When Theo is here, there is no fear.' He kept on saying that and then decided to do a U-turn. He made a mistake and went off the dirt road into the farm that was flooded, and when he realised how soft the mud was, he put his foot down flat on the accelerator and went straight into the farm, sinking more and more. As the wheels spun making a horrible noise, I said to him, *'Thame se thelo gavoora, na drappias da garvoona.'* When the engine stalled in the middle of the farm, we laughed our heads off until the other boys came to our rescue.

Moral
If you brag, one day you will be caught.

8. Thaskale boo thithaskes', je nomon then egrades.
8. Δάσκαλε που δίδασκες τζαι νόμον εν εκράτες.
8. Teacher, practise what you preach.

Meaning
Practise what you preach.

Used
Used when someone preaches others to do the right thing but doesn't do it himself/herself.

Example
When one tells everyone that smoking is bad for them and yet one smokes, you say, *'Thaskale boo thithaskes', je nomon then egrades.'*

Moral
Show others by example.

*9. Thig**on** moo ya**oo**rin, **o**bos th**e**lo thinno do.*
9. Δικό μου γαούριν, όπου θέλω διννω το.
9. My donkey, I tie it my way.

Meaning
With my property I can do what I like.

Used
Used when one tells you how to conduct your affairs.

Example
Jovanni fitted an ugly rusty roof rack on his car because he found it a bargain at a garage sale. All his friends told him that he spoilt the looks of his car, but he didn't care; his answer was '*Thig**on** moo ya**oo**rin, **o**bos th**e**lo thinno do.*' Fair enough.

Moral
Handle your affairs the way you see fit.

10. Thos moo jira don andran soo, je soo ame na vris allon.
10. Δώσ'μου τζυρά τον αντρα σου τζαι σου αμε νάβρεις άλλον.
10. Lady, give me your husband, and you go seek another.

Meaning
One has the audacity to ask you for something of yours (as important as your wife) that one knows you need and use all the time.

Used
Used when one has the audacity to ask you for something important that you need and use all the time.

Example
Thomas, my neighbour, asked me to let him use my garage so he could park his new car in it. I said, 'But I use it for my car.' He said, 'Your car is old, and you can park it outside in your driveway.' I was stunned to hear that and said, 'Are you crazy? *Thos moo jira don andran soo, je soo ame na vris allon.*'

Moral
Be kind but not stupid.

The audacity of some people goes beyond logic.

V

1. Vaose je Romanise j'obothhen thhelis emba.
1. Βάωσε τζαι ρομάνισε τζ' όποθθεν θέλεις έμπα,
1. Lock-up the house and walk in from anywhere.

Meaning
You lock the door, and yet one can get in from anywhere else.

Used
Used when one locks the door when others can easily have access from elsewhere.

Example
Andrikko was closing up shop the other day; the doors and gates were quite flimsy. I said to him, '*Vaose je romanise je **o**bothhen thhelis **e**mba.*'

He said, 'Don't worry, I have the dog loose.'

Moral
There is no point in locking up if one can walk in from anywhere else.

2. Valli boo d'onan je vkalli boo d'allon.
2. Βάλλει που τόναν τζαι φκάλλει που τάλλον.
2. In from one ear and out the other.

Meaning
The person you talk to doesn't take any notice.

Used
Used when one is not interested to pay attention to what you say.

Example
The teacher told the students repeatedly to pay attention because the topic they were discussing was very important and concerned every one of them. He continued with his lecture and saw that some students weren't paying attention. At the end he called them to answer some questions, and of course, they had no idea. Then he said, 'I warned you, but *vallis boo d'onan je vkallis boo d'allon.*'

Moral
To make a point ensure you get the attention.

3. Vkenni bobano san do lain.
3. Φκέννει πουπάνω σαν το λάϊν.
3. Rises on top, like oil.

Meaning
Even when one is wrong, one still wins the argument and comes up on top like oil.

Used
Used when a manipulative person is wrong and still manages to win the argument.

Example
Constantinos was a gambler, who had a small business in town. He would go home very late, and his wife was not very happy about it. He was such a smooth-talker that he always managed to convince her that he was working late. One night she was waiting for him to come home until 1 a.m., when she decided to call him. She called the office, and there was no answer. She then decided to take a drive downtown to the casino where he usually gambled. She went upstairs and saw him gambling but kept her distance, trying to figure out what to do. Then she called him on his mobile and asked him where he was.

He replied, 'What sort of question is that? You know I am at work, working very hard.' She was shaking but gathered all the strength she could and said, 'You are a liar!' He quickly replied, 'How dare you question me?'

She said, 'Because I am watching you playing cards standing in the corner!'

He paused for a minute and then got up and walked up to her, and in a very intimidating tone of voice, he said, 'How dare you come here, this time of the night? What sort of wife are you to spy on your husband, to come and humiliate me like this in front of my friends? I will never forgive you for that.' He made her feel so guilty that she apologised to him and went home crying. Then Bappoo said, *'Vkenni bobano san do lain.'*

Moral
Beware of manipulative people.

4. *Vlebis thki**o** je en mall**o**nnoon, eksere boss en boos don **e**nan.*
4. Βλέιπρεις δκιο τζ' εν μαλλώνουν,
έξερε πΔως εν που τον νεαν.
4. If a couple don't quarrel, it is because of the one.

Meaning
If a couple is getting on well, it is because one of them is more tolerant and gives in for the sake of peace.

Used
Used usually as a complaint by the one that gives in.

Example
We went to visit Kevin and his wife Denise the other day to wish them happy fiftieth anniversary. Kevin is not a very talkative person, but when he was asked about his secret for being married for so long, he replied, 'It's very simple. I used the *"yes, dear"* method and never had an argument.'

That's when Bappoo says, '*Vlebis thki**o** je en mall**o**nnoon, eksere boss en boo don **e**nan.*'

Moral
When one gives in, there is always peace at home.

(It might not be fair for one, but is peaceful.)

5. *Voor**a**, je en siftanni.*
5. Βουρά τζ' εν συφταίννει.
5. Bursting and running.

Meaning
One runs as if one had diarrhoea and has to rush to the toilet quickly.

Used
Used when one runs like crazy to make it on time, because one left things to the last minute.

Example
Andrew was getting married in two weeks' time. Despite all the reminders from Eleni, his fiancé, to organise his wedding suit, he kept postponing it until the last minute.

He was a tall man, and it was very hard to find a suit his size. The only alternative was to have it tailor-made. He only had one week left before the wedding, so he was running around like mad to find a tailor that could do it on time. Eventually he found one, but he said he was very busy. Andrew then put an envelope with fifty euros in his hand and he said, 'Ah. Well, we would have to jump the queue and finish it on time, won't we?'

'Of course,' said the tailor. 'You can pick it up on Friday.' He went home exhausted, and Eleni said, 'Now, *vooras je en siftannis* Why did you leave it to the last minute?'

Moral
Don't leave things to the last minute.

6. *Voon**on** me voon**on** en ism**ii**.*
6. Βουνόν με βουνόν εν ησμίει.
6. Two mountains do not meet.

Meaning
Only two mountains can't meet; everything else is possible.

Used
Used when old friends meet unexpectedly after many years.

Example
I was in a Greek confectionery shop on Lonsdale Street, Melbourne, a few years ago. I was having a cup of coffee and a baklava with some friends. I was looking at the door and saw a two elderly ladies coming in. One of them, the tall, skinny one, seemed familiar to me.

They took a seat opposite us, and the waiter gave them the menu.

I overheard the other lady calling her Stella, and I tried to remember where I knew her from, but I couldn't. After they had their coffees, she called the waiter and asked him for something; it was then that I recognised her voice. My favourite arts teacher. I got up, walked up to her, put my arm on her shoulder, and said, 'Yiasou, ayapi mou (Hi, darling).'

She leant back, looked at me, and said, 'Do I know you?'

I said, 'The last time you saw me, I had lots of hair in 1966, and I was calling you pussy cat.'

She said, 'Oh my God, Thimitrakis!' She jumped up, and we hugged and kissed and cried, and then she introduced me to her friend as her best student. I invited them to my home to meet my family, but they said they were on the way to the airport, going back home after three weeks' holiday in Australia. She said that I was the last person she expected to meet in Australia because she knew I was in South Africa.

I said, *'Voonon me voonon en ismii.'*

Moral
You never know who you might run into.

7. Vlebe erga k'ohi loyia.
7. Βλέπε έργα τζ' όϊ λόγια.
7. See action not talk.

English version: All talk but no action.

Meaning
People usually talk just for the sake of having a conversation.

If it's important to us, we should only take notice of their actions and not their words.

Used
Used when talkers say, 'I will, I can, or I am going to do this,' but nothing ever eventuates.

Example
I bumped into Arthur the other day at Victoria Market and asked how they were doing at work. He was a production manager for a large component manufacturer. He said, 'Same shit, different day.' I said, 'What do you mean?' He said, 'We have a meeting once a week with all managers. We all take up a task to do for the week. Most of them, usually the boss's pets, are the first ones to put their hand up and say, 'Me! I'll do this, I can do that, I can do this,' but by the following week, they do absolutely nothing, except giving a load of excuses and blaming others. Last week I handed in my resignation and told the boss, '*Vlebe erga ke ohi loyia.* I have had enough of promises.'

Moral
Take notice of what people do, not what they say.

8. Voora na deliosis j'ade na da mballosis.
8. Βούρα να τελιώσεις τζαι άτε να τα μπαλλώσεις.
8. Rush to finish and sit to repair.

Meaning
If you are in a hurry to finish something, usually you miss something or you make a mistake and have to do it again.

Used
Used when one rushes to do something quickly, and stuffs up.

Example
Xenis and Adamos were kitchen cabinet installers. They were working on a kitchen one day and they were rushing to finish before the weekend so they could go fishing. The boss told them to take care because they were handling expensive and fragile units. Of course, they didn't listen. They damaged one of the hi-gloss emporite finished doors, and then they called the boss and told him.

He hit the roof and said, 'It's Friday today, and I needed to get paid so I can pay you people as well. Now I won't get paid, you won't get paid, and we'll have to repair the door and go back on Monday again! *Voora na deliosis jade na da mballosis.*'

Moral
Don't rush. Take your time and do it properly.

1. Yidon eshis, Thheon eshis.
1. Γείτον έσιεις, Θεόν έσιεις.
1. You have a good neighbour, you have God.

Meaning
It is good to have a good neighbour you can rely on for any help or emergency.

Used
Used to express the importance of having a good neighbour.

Example
One night the telephone rang at three o'clock in the morning. I picked it up, and it was the young girl that lived by herself next door. She was terrified and said, 'Jim, someone is trying to break into the house.'

I quickly put my pants on and rushed next door. We checked all around, and all was clear. She said, 'I heard the noise at the gate.'

I went and checked the gate and found that the hinges were loose and with a little breeze it would make noise.

I secured it temporarily, and everything was okay.

She thanked me and said, *'Yidon eshis, Thheon eshis.'*

Moral
It's very important that you are in good terms with your neighbour.

2. Yia do hattirin dis vasilijias, binni i ylastra do neron.
2. Για το χαττίριν της βασιλιτσιάς πίννει η γλάστρα το νερό.
2. For basil's sake, you water the pot.

Meaning
Your intention is to water the basil, but the pot drinks as well.

Used
Used when you tolerate certain situations for the sake of someone or something else.

Example
One doesn't get on with his mother in law, but he tolerates a lot of things because he doesn't like to upset his wife. Bappoo says, '*Yia do hattirin dis vasilijias, binni i ylastra do neron.*'

Moral
Sometimes we need to make compromises for something or someone we value.

3. Yiat'en thigon doo kavki don, yiati do rizi kshi don.
3. Γιατί εν δικόν του καύκει τον, γιατί το ρίζει ξιεί τον.
3. Because it's his, it burns him, and because he owns it, he cares.

Meaning
One only cares about one's own possessions.

Used
Used when one takes proper care when it comes to one's own property.

Example
John was driving his own car for a few days until the company's car was repaired. He refused to take it on dirt roads or load it heavily, because it was his own, and he wanted to look after it. It can be said, '*Yiat'en thigon doo kavki don, yiati doh rizi kshi don.*'

Moral
Look after things that you use, especially when you don't own them.

*4. Yia mig**ros** mig**ros** band**re**ftoo, yia mig**ros** galoi**re**ftoo.*
4. Για μικρός-μικρός παντρεύτου για μικρός καλοηρεύτου.
4. Get married young, or become a monk young.

Meaning
Traditionally, people believed that it is important to get married and have a family while you are still young and energetic and have children to grow up with you.

Used
Used to stress the importance of early marriage to the young ones.

Example
Many times we have conversations with young family friends, particularly the girls, about family planning. I believe that the younger you have children, the lower the risk of having health problems and complications, and you don't have to be a gynaecologist to know that. Of course, there are exceptions, but you can't make decisions based on exceptions.

I remember one night we were watching one of the doctor's shows on TV, and the doctor said that as the women grow older, their ovulation is affected. They produce less and less eggs, and they could have more problems and less chance of conceiving. My little boy then asked why they don't go to the supermarket to get some. His mum said, 'They are different eggs, darling.' He then asked, 'What's the difference, Mum?'

I said, 'They are free range.'

Anyway, back to the serious note. My wife and I got married young and if we had to do it again, we would do exactly the same, as *'Yia migros migros bandreftoo, yia migros galoireftoo.'*

One important aspect of starting a family young is not only that you are doing what nature intended, but also the physical aspect. It takes an enormous amount of effort and energy to raise children properly, which, of course, gets depleted as we get older. How good would it be to grow up with your kids while you have lots of energy and are there for them?

My wife and I got married young and if I had to do it again I would do exactly the same thing.

Moral
The younger you start a family, the more natural it is.

5. Yia don psillon egapsan do babloman.
5. Για τον ψύλλον εκάψαν το πάπλωμα.
5. For a nit they burn the doona.

Meaning

The amount of effort one puts into a project outweighs by far the benefits.

Used

Used when one uses wrong methods to solve a little problem, and as a result of that, the expense outweighs the benefit.

Example

Nastradin Hodjia planted a plum tree near the entrance of his house. Every time he came home with his donkey, the donkey would quickly have a quick bite on it. Hodjia was infuriated by this and hit the donkey with a stick to teach him a lesson, but to no avail. The next day the same thing happened, only this time Hodjia hit him with an axe on the head, because the stick wasn't working. His wife came out and saw the donkey on the floor taking his last breaths and said, 'You killed the poor animal.'

His replied, 'Well, I had to teach him a lesson.'

Then his wife said, *'Yia don psillon egapses do babloman.* How cruel can you get?'

Moral

Ill-considered solutions are counterproductive.

6. *Yia na se bethhim**oo**sin,* ***a****rke llion na se th**oo**sin.*
6. Για να σε πεθυμούσιν, άρκε λλίο να σε δούσιν.
6. If you want them to miss you, see them rarely.

Meaning
If you want people to miss you, don't spend too much time with them.

Used
Used when one becomes a burden with frequent and long visits.

Example
The mother-in-law loved her grandkids and went nearly every night to see them. She wasn't the easiest person to get along with, and the daughter-in-law was getting a bit upset. The father-in-law then said, '*Yi**a** na se bethhim**oo**sin,* ***a****rke llion na se th**oo**sin.*'

Moral
Respect the privacy of others.

7. Yleboo na se glebi jo Thheos.
7. Γλέπου να σε γλέπει τζ' ο Θεός.
7. God will protect you if you protect yourself.

Meaning
Look after yourself if you want God tolook after you.

Used
Used when one blames God for not being protective during an incident.

Example
The Religous Fisherman

This reminds me of the story of a very religious fisherman who was in the bay fishing in his little boat. Suddenly a strong wind caused the sea to get choppy, and as it was worsening, a huge fishing trawler appeared; the captain called out to him, 'Tie your boat on! You cannot sail in that tiny boat!' He replied, 'No, thanks, I am okay. God Loves me, and he will protect me.' The trawler disappeared.

An hour passed, and by now the waves were so high that he was losing control. As he was struggling to steer his dingy in the right direction, another cruiser appeared out of the fog. They also called him to get on board to be rescued, but, stubborn as he was, he yelled back, 'Thank you, but I am okay. God loves me, and he will look after me.' They didn't argue with him either and sailed on.

By now the waves were going over the little boat, and suddenly the horn of a huge tanker made him jump, but despite the offer from the crew to help him, he still refused to accept help saying the same thing that he was okay, God was was with him, and he didn't need them. So they left. Not long after, a huge wave capsized the tiny boat, and there he was, hanging on the edge of the boat. Hungry and exhausted, he tried to swim ashore, but the waves swirled him to the bottom of the ocean and drowned him. When he arrived at the Pearly Gates up in heaven, the first thing he did was to go straight to Saint Peter to complain that he had trusted God, but God let him down. Saint Peter then replied, 'You idiot, God sent you help three times, but you refused to accept it!'

Moral
Look after yourself, and God will help you.

8. Yiorti moo emenan, baramoni thiki soo.
8. Γιορτή μου εμένα, παραμονή δική σου.
8. My celebration, the eve of yours.

Meaning

What happened to me today will happen to you tomorrow.

Used

Used as a warning to others that what happens to us today can happen to them tomorrow and not to make comments that they might regret later.

Example

Yorkis's daughter fell pregnant by a boy from school and was the talk of the town. Ironically, some of the parents that gossiped copped the same thing later, and Yorkis said, '*Yiorti moo emenan, baramoni thiki soo.*'

Moral

Don't judge something for which you might be judged upon tomorrow.

The Ioannou bunch reunion in 1983. The boys, back row from left: John, Kyriakos, Stelios and Jim; second row: the wives Nancy, Avra, Mum, and Dad (Hristalleni and Giannaros and Giorgoulla and Irene. Front: little Natasa, Christalene, Christalleni, Iakovos, and Angelo.

Index

Proverbs – ΠΑΡΟΙΜΙΕΣ

A

Page 3 to 90

1. *Agooe yeroo simvoolin, je bethevmenoo ynosin.*
Ακουε γέρου συμβουλήν τζαι παιδευμένου γνώσην.
Take old man's advice and academic's knowledge.

2. *Aboo libade doo gattoo do lardin, dron da rooha doo i bondiji.*
Απού λυπάται του κάττου το λαρτίν τρών τα ρούχα του οι ποντιτζοί.
If you don't feed the cat, your clothes will be eaten by mice.

3. *Anifandaris ditsiros, tsangaris alibolidos.*
Ανυφαντάρης (υφαντης, ράφτης) τίτσιρος, τσαγκάρης αλυπόλητος.
Naked tailor, barefoot shoemaker.

4. *Avoolos noos, gamni din dihin yierimin.*
Αβουλος νους κάμνει την τύχην γέρημη.
Illogical decisions bring misfortune.

5. *Avraon ambelin en doos yatharoos mandra.*
Αβρανον αμπέλι εν τους γαδάρους μάντρα.
Open vineyard, donkey's stall.

6. *Anayios don gollion na soo vgali da mmathkia soo.*
Ανάγιως τον κολιόν να σου φκάλει τα μάθκια.
Nurture the jackdaw to poke your eyes out.

7. *Anaelasen ei eyia dis gooellas.*
Αναέλασεν η αίγια της κουέλλας.
The goat mocked the sheep.

8. *Ab**oo** bell**on** je b**oo** mitsin, na m**a**thhis din alithkian.*
Από πελλόν τζαι που μιτσήν να μάθεις την αλήθκειαν.
You learn the truth from a fool or a child.

9. *Ab**oo** boni ba sdon yiadr**on**.*
Από πονεί πα στο γιατρόν.
Who has the pain goes to the doctor.

10. *Ab**on** appekso doo hor**oo**, kseri boll**a** dra**oo**thkia.*
Από απέξω του χορού, ξέρει πολλά τραούθκια.
Who is not on the dance floor knows all the songs.

11. *Ab**on** ag**oo**i doo yoni**oo**, bara yoni**a**s jim**a**de.*
Από ακούει του γονιού, παραγωνιάς τζοιμάται.
Who doesn't take advice from parents ends up in the streets.

12. *Ab**on** andrebede, o cosm**os** en thik**os** doo.*
Από αντρέπεται ο κόσμος εν δικός του.
Who feels no embarassement owns the world.

13. *Ab**oo** varig**oo**f**a** dergazi.*
Από βαρυκουφά, ταιρκάζει τα.
Who has hearing loss rhymes own words.

14. *Athkiaser**os** bab**a**s thh**a**vki je doos zondan**oo**s.*
Αδκιασερός παπάς, θάφκει τζαι τους ζωντανούς.
Priest that's not busy buries people alive.

15. *Ag**oo**e boll**a** je bistevke lli**a**.*
Ακουε πολλά τζαι πίστευκε λλία.
Listen to a lot, believe a few.
English version: **Don't believe everything you hear.**

16. *Alla lo**y**ia thhki**e** bab**a**.*
Αλλα λόγια θκε παπά.
Why the priest changed the subject.

17. *Allaksen o Manolios, Je evalen da rooha doo alios.*
Αλλαξεν ο Μανωλιός τζ' έβαλεν τα ρούχα του αλλοιώς.
Manuel dressed differently now.

18. *Alla enda mmathkia doo laoo, je alla doo gookoofkiaoo.*
Αλλα εν τα μμάθκια του λαού τζι άλλα του κουκκουφκιάου.
The eyes of the owl are one thing, and the eyes of the hare are another.

19. *Alli spernoon je thherizoon, Je alli dron je magarizoon.*
Αλλοι σπέρνουν τζαι θερίζουν τζι άλλοι τρων τζαι μακαρίζουν.
Some do the sowing and harvesting, and others get the crop.

20. *Ama thipsa i avli soo, men shienonnis do neron se ksenes avles.*
Αμα διψά η αυλή σου, μεν σιονώννεις το νερό σε ξένες αυλές.
If your garden is dry, don't pour the water in other gardens.

21. *Ammen lathkiasis don drohon, en yirizi.*
Αμμέν λαθκιάσεις τον τροχόν, εν γυρίζει.
The wheel will not turn if you don't lubricate it.

22. *Ama en bai o Moameth sto voonon, bai do voonon is don Moameth.*
Αμαν εν πάει ο Μωάμεθ στο βουνό, πάει το βουνό στον Μωάμεθ.
If Mohammed doesn't go to the mountain, the mountain goes to Mohammed.

23. *An ekseres din bedran boo idan na goodsoovlisis, eboirizes din.*
Αν έξερες την πέτραν πούταν να κουτσουβλίσεις, επογύριζες την.
If you knew the stone you tripped on, you would have avoided it.

24. *Abon imbori na theri don yaron, thernni do saman.*
Απόν ημπορεί να δέρει τον γάρον, δέρνει το σάμα.
Who can't beat the donkey beats the saddle.
English equivalent: **Who can't kill the king kills the messenger.**

25. *Abo shi thendron, eshi oshion.*
Απόσιει δέντρον έσιει οσσιόν.
Who has a tree has shade.

26. *Abon eshi noon, eshi bothkia.*
Απόνεσιει νουν, έσιει πόδκια.
Who doesn't have brains has feet.

27. *Abo shi mooyian, mooyiazete.*
Απόσιει μούγιαν, μουγιάζεται.
Who has a fly gets annoyed.

28. *Arhi horis delos, anofeli.*
Αρχή χωρίς τέλος, ανώφελη.
It's pointless to start and not finish.

29. *Akooe meyalon thendron, je berne mitsin galathin.*
Ακου μεγάλο δέντρον τζι έπερνε μιτζίν καλάθι.
When you hear of a large tree, take small basket.

30. *Alli psihomahoon, je alli gavlomahoon.*
Αλλοι ψυχομαχούν τζι άλλοι καβλομαχούν.
Some are dying, and others want sex.

31. Astia, astia, ma aggastrothika.
Αστεία Αστεία, μα αγγαστρώθηκα.
Joking joking, but I got pregnant.

32. *Ama eshis dethkioos filoos, inda thelis doos ohtroos.*
Αμαν έσιεις τέθκιους φίλους, ήντα θέλεις τους οχτρούς.
With friends like these, you don't need enemies.

33. *Ama miniskis se yiallenon spidin, men bedassis betres.*
Αν μεινίσκεις σε γυάλλενο σπίτι, μεν πετάσσεις πέτρες.
If you live in a glass house, don't throw stones.

34. *Ama vlepis din goofin, men yirevkis din golosirmathkian dis.*
Αμα δεις τήν κουφή μέν γυρεύκεις την κωλοσυρμαθκιάν της.
If you see the snake, don't look for its tail.

35. *Amm'en glapsi doe moron, i mana en do daizi.*
Αμμέν κλάψει το μωρό, η μάμα εν το ταΐζει.
If the baby doesn't cry, its mother won't feed it.

36. *Amm'en ispiris, en thherizis.*
Αμμέν ησπύρεις εν θερίζεις.
If you don't sow, you don't reap.

37. *Athe befkoos yia ilarka.*
Αδε πεύκους για υλάρκα!
These pine trees are good for sieve rings.

38. *Aboo ssothgiazi endega je boo ksothgiazi thega,
en athrobos doo haircoo je thosde doo yienegan.*
Απού σωδκιάζει έντεκα τζι απού ξοδκιάζει δέκα.
Εν άθθρωπος του χαϊρκού τζαι δώστε του γεναίκα.
He who spends less than he earns prospers and deserves a wife.

39. *Allin mas ethiksen je allin mas embiksen.*
Άλλην μας έδειξεν τζι άλλην μας έμπηξεν.
He showed us one and pricked us with another.

40. *Andan na psorkasi o yidos sou, je esoo votanin yirevke.*
Αμαν ψωρκάσει ο γείτος σου, τζ' εσού βοτάνι γύρευκε.
When your neighbour catches scab, look for a remedy too.

41. *Aboo ayaba, bethevki.*
Απ αγαπα πεδευκει.
He who cares for you counsels you.
English: **Be cruel to be kind.**

42. *Aryia midir basis kakias.*
Αργία, μήτηρ πάσης κακίας.
Lazing idle mother of all evil.

43. *Agapa don filon sou, me da elattomada doo.*
Αγάπα τον φίλο σου με τα ελαττώματα του.
Love your friend with his faults.

44. *Abon d'areskoon oi sfirkes en ba ston goomothromon.*
Απόν τ' αρέσκουν οι σφυρκές, εν πα στον κωμοδρόμο.
Who doesn't like hammering doesn't go to the blacksmith.

45. *Akoma en don ithamen je Yiannin don evkalamen.*
Ακόμα εν τον είδαμε τζαι Γιάννην τον εφκάλαμε.
We haven't seen him yet and named him Yanni.

46. *Ashimofore je men rrias.*
Ασσιημοφόρε τζαι μεν ριάς.
Dress badly and feel warm.

47. *Athrobos agrammados, ksilon abelejidon.*
Αδρωπος αγράμματος, ξύλον απελέτζητον.
Uneducated person, uncarvable hard wood.

48. *Abou berna je ellali me yiasoo me galos don, sto panairin ebardon jeosa soo thosoon thos don.*
Απου περνα τζιαι εν λαλει με γεια σου με καλως τον, στο παναηριν επαρτον τζαι οσα σου δωσουν δως τον.
Who passes and doesn't greet is not a respectful person.

B

Page 91 to 111

1. *Ban medron ariston.* (By the Greek Philosopher Diogenes Laertius).
Παν μέτρον άριστον.
Everything in moderation.

2. *Bes moo me bioos bas, na soo bo bios ise.*
Πες μου με ποιούς πας, να σου πω ποιός εισαι.
Tell me who your friends are, and I'll tell you who you are.

3. *Bera vreshi, stin Karamanian shionizi.*
Πέρα βρέσιει, στην Καραμανιά σιονίζει.
It's raining overseas and snowing on Mount Karamania (in Turkey).

4. *Bebse don bell**o**n, je l**a**mne dabis**o**n do.*
Πέψε τον πελλόν τζαι λάμνε ταπισόν του.
Send a fool and go after him.

5. *Bell**oo** Je ay**i**oo men daksis.*
Πελλού τζ' αγίου μεν τάξεις.
Do not promise a saint or a fool.

6. *B**e**rnise stin vrisin Je f**e**rnise **a**bodon.*
Πέρνει σε στη βρύση τζιαι φέρνει σε άποτον.
Takes you to the water and brings you back thirsty.

7. *Bed**a**ssi **o**fkera, na b**a**ri yiem**a**da.*
Πετάσσει όφκαιρα, να παρει γεμάτα.
Throws empty ones to get full ones.

8. *Bodavristoo **o**spoo ftannis.*
Ποταβρίστου ώσπου φτάννεις.
Stretch as far as you can reach.

9. *B**oo** loodoorg**a** thki**o** eklishi**e**s, b**a**nda dis mias yiel**a** dis.*
Πού λουτουρκά δκιο εκκλησιές, πάντα της μιας γελά της.
Who preaches in two churches doesn't do justice to one.

10. *Boo jini**a** thki**o** la**oo**s, h**a**nni doos je doos thki**o**.*
Πού τζυνιά δκιο λαούς, χάννει τους τζαι τους δκιο.
Who hunts two hares at the same time loses them both.

11. *Boo don sian**o**n bodam**o**n na foase.*
Που τον σιανόν ποταμόν να φοάσαι.
Beware of the slow-flowing creek.

12. *Boo **i**soun b**oo**bode.*
Που ήσουν, πούποτε.
Where were you? Nowhere.
English equivalent: **Back to square one.**

13. *Bolidehnidis ke erimospidis.*
Πολυτεχνίτης τζαι ερημοσπίτης.
Man of all trades lives in ruins.
English: **Jack of all trades, master of none.**

14. *Boo stillon stillon anesin, osboo na vki i psishi doo.*
Που στύλλον-στύλλον άνεσην, ώσπου να βκει η ψυσιή του.
From post to post grasping a breath, until death.

D

Page 113 to 131

1. *Da bolla loyia eftoshia.*
Τα πολλά λόγια εν φτώσια.
Too much talk is misery.

2. *Doo fronimoo do bethi, brin binasi mayirevi.*
Του φρονίμου το παιδί πριν πεινάσει μαϊρέφκει.
Sensible people cook before they get hungry.

3. *Do thendron boo lia, en ispazi.*
Το δέντρον που λυά εν ισπάζει.
The tree that bends doesn't snap.

4. *Do eksibnon boollin, boo din moottin biannede.*
Το έξυπνον πουλλίν που τη μούττην πιάνεται.
The smart bird gets caught by its beak.

5. *Do shinin doo horkadi monon en eftannen, je thiblon ftanni je berissevgi.*
Το σιηνίν του χωρκάτη μονόν εν έφταννεν τζαι διπλόν φτάννει τζαι Περισσεύκει.
The villager's rope was too short when single, but more than long enough when doubled.

6. *Do shillin soo je do bethin soo, obos da mathis.*
Το σιυλλί σου τζαι το παιδί σου όπως τα μάθεις.
Your puppy and your kid behave as you train them.

7. *Do min se melli min rodas.*
Το μη σε μέλλει μη ρωτάς.
Do not ask if it doesn't concern you.

8. *Do yinadin vkalli ammadin.*
Το γινάτι φκάλλει αμμάτι.
Stubbornness costs you an eye.

9. *Dravame je as gleo.*
Τράβα με τζ' ας κλαίω.
I refuse but force me.
English equivalent: **Twist my arm.**

E

Page 133 to 170

1. *Em mitsis amman rotsis.*
Εν μιτσής αμμάν ροτσίς.
He is little, but tough.

2. *Epien o ftohos na armasti, je mitchanen ei nihta.*
Επήεν ο φτωχός ν' αρμαστεί τζ' εμίτσιανεν η νύχτα.
The poor went to get married, and the night shrank.

3. *Evalan mas da thkio mas bothkia se enan babootsin.*
Εβάλαν μας τα δκιο μας πόδκια σ' ένα παπούτσι.
They squeezed both of our feet in one shoe.
Similar to: **They made us tighten our belts.**

4. *Evcalen onoman o theristis je eppesen je jimadoon.*
Εφκαλεν όνομαν ο θεριστής τζ' έππεσεν τζαι τζοιμάτουν.
The reaper made a name and couldn't care less.

5. *Evcalen i glossa moo mallia.*
Εφκαλεν η γλώσσα μου μαλιά.
Hair grew on my tongue.

6. *Evkiges sdon horon, brebi na horepsis.*
Εφκήκες στο χορόν πρέπει να χορέψεις.
When you get on the dance floor, you must dance.

7. *Elimbisen i rka sta sica, je enna fa je da sicofilla.*
Ελίμπησεν η ρκα στα σύκα τζ' εννά φα τζαι τα συκόφυλλα.
The old lady loved the figs so much that she would even eat the leaves.

8. *Enan shelionin en ferni din anniksin.*
Ενα σιελιόνιν εν φέρνει την άννοιξη.
One swallow doesn't bring spring.

9. *Enen da rasa boo camnoon don baban, en o babas boo camni da rasa.*
Εννεν τα ράσα που κάμνουν τον παπάν, εν ο παπάς που κάμνει τα ράσα.
The gown doesn't make the priest; it's the priest that makes the gown.

10. *Eminamen san eminen, o Hajimarcos bersi, elipsandon da garvoona je enishen na thoolepsi.*
Εμείναμεν σαν έμεινεν ο Χατζημάρκος πέρσυ, ελείψαν τον τα καρβουνα τζ' ένεισιεν να δουλέψει.
We got stranded like Hajimarcos did last year, when he ran out of coal.

11. *En me da hronia boo gadevenni o noos.*
Εν με τα χρόνια που κατεβαίνει ο νους.
Maturity comes with age.

12. *En mathimena da voona boo da shionia.*
Εν μαθημένα τα βουνά που σιόνια.
The mountains are used to the snow.

13. Egamenda shionin je yastrin.
Εκαμεν τα σιόνιν τζαι γαστρίν.
Stuffed everything up.

14. Ebian je da avga je do kalathin.
Επήαν τζαι τ' αυκά τζαι το καλάθι.
All gone the eggs and the basket.

15. Ebien yia mallin je irten gooremenos.
Επήε για μαλλίν τζαι ήρτεν κουρεμένος.
Went for hair and returned with his hair cut.

16. Etho karavia hannonde, je i jira htenizede.
Εδώ καράβκια χάννουνται τζαι η τζυρά χτενίζεται.
The ship is sinking, and madam is brushing her hair.

17. Efaamen don voon, Je eminen mas o nooros.
Εφάαμεν τον βουν τζ' έμεινεν μας ο νούρος.
We ate the whole ox but the tail.

18. *Ecamen don psillon gamilon.*
Εκαμεν το ψύλλον κάμηλον.
He made a camel out of a nit.

19. En o yaros doo Hodjia, boo don emathhen na men droi.
Εν ο γάρος του Χότζια που τον έμαθεν να μεν τρώει.
Hodjia's donkey trained not to eat.

20. Evalan don aloobon na ylebi des ornithes.
Εβάλαν τον αλουπόν να βλέπει τες όρνιθες.
They put a fox to guard the hen house.

21. Evalen don nooron doo mes d'ashielia doo.
Εβαλεν τον νούρον του μεσ' τα σιέλια του.
He put his tail between his legs.

22. *Eyio straonno je boolo je soo amblebe je yoraze.*
Εγιώ στραώννω τζαι πουλώ τζ' εσού άμπλεψε τζαι γόραζε.
I blind you and sell, and you look and buy.

23. *En oksina da stafilia, elalen i alooboo boo en daftannen.*
Εν οξυνα τα σταφυλια, ελαλεν ι αλουπου που εν τα εφταννεν.
The fox couldn't reach the grapes and said they were sour.

24. *Ela bappoo, na soo thikso dambelia soo.*
Ελα παππού να σου δείξω τ' αμπέλια σου.
Grandpa, let me show you your vineyards.

25. *Egilisen do stooppoman je ivren do lavezin.*
Ετζύλησεν το στούππωμα τζαι ήβρεν το λαβέζι.
The lid found its pot.

26. *Etsi kkelle, etsi kshioorafin theli.*
Ετσι κκελλέ, έτσι ξιουράφι θέλει.
Such a head needs such a shaver.
English version: **You were asking for it**, or **You deserve everything you get.**

F

Page 171 to 178

1. *Fain na famen eneshi, Je theloomen rebanakia yia oreksin.*
Φαΐν να φάμεν εν έσιει τζαι θέλουμεν ρεπανάκια για όρεξη.
If you don't have food, you look for appetisers.

2. *Fteon doo da rooha doo.*
Φταίουν του τα ρούχα του.
He is so moody, he blames his clothes.

3. *Fakkoon doo baba meh da brosfora.*
Φακκούν του παπά με τα πρόσφορα.
They hit the priest with the votive bread.

4. *Filae da rooha soo, nahis da misa.*
Φύλαε τα ρούχα σου νάσιεις τα μισά.
If you safeguard your clothes, you lose only half of them.

G

Page 179 to 196

1. *Gootsi stravi ston Ain Bandeleimonan.*
Κουτσοί, στραβοί στον Αην Παντελεήμονα.
Lame and blind, going to Saint Pandeleimon.

2. *Galeston is don yamon soo, na soo bi je abo hronoo.*
Κάλεστον στον γάμο σου να σου πει τζαι του χρόνου.
Invite one to your wedding to wish you to get married again next year.

3. *Galion arya bara bode.*
Κάλιον αργά παρά ποτέ.
Better late than never.

4. *Galion yaooro thinne bara yaooro yirevke.*
Κάλιον γαουρόδιννε παρά γαουρογύρευκε.
Better tie the donkey now than look for it later.

5. *Galion enan je sto sherin, bara thega je garterin.*
Κάλιον ένα τζαι στο σιέριν παρά δέκα τζαι καρτέρει.
Better one in hand than ten and wait.
English equivalent: **Better the egg now than the chicken later.**

6. *Gallittera na soo vki do madin bara to onoman.*
Καλλίττερα να σου φκεί το μάτι παρά το όνομα.
Better to lose an eye than your name.

7. *Galos – galos o shiros mas, evkiken halaziaris.*
Καλός-καλός ο σιοίρος μας έφκηκεν χαλαζιάρης.
Our best pig turned out to have a disease.

8. *Gamila glanni sto Bendagomon.*
Καμήλα κλάννει στο Πεντάκωμο.
Camel farts in Bendagomo (village).

9. *Gatse yare psofa osti na vki drifillin.*
Κάτσε γάρε ψώφα όστι να φκεί το τριφύλλι.
Sit and die, donkey, until the clover grows.

10. *Gitakse din gambooran soo, brin na bis yia don allon.*
Κοίταξε την καμπούρα σου, πρν να πεις για τον άλλον.
Look at your own hump before you criticise others.

11. *Goronos goronoo, mmadin enivgalli.*
Κόρονος κορόνου αμμάτιν εν ηφκάλλει.
One magpie doesn't harm another.

12. *Gootshia je gologasin, enan dobon en na basin.*
Κουτσιά τζαι κολοκάσι έναν τόπον εννά πάσι.
Broad beans and gologasi going into the same place.

H

Page 197 to 199

1. *Horevke jira Maroo, ma'shie je enian doo moroo.*
Χόρευκε τζυρά Μαρού μα' σιε τζ' έγνοιαν του μωρού.
You can dance, Mrs Marou, but keep an eye on the baby too.

I

Page 201 to 228

1. *I Athina se voitha, an valis esoo shierin.*
Η Αθηνά σε βοηθά, αν βαλεις εσού σιηεριν.
Goddess Athena helps you if you use your hands.
Ancient Greek: Sin Athena ke hira kini

2. *I gooza bai bolles fores stin vrisin, amma gabode spazi.*
Η κούζα πάει πολλές φορές στη βρύσην, αμμά κάποτε σπάζει.
The pot goes to the fountain many times, but one day it smashes.

3. *I bolli thoolia droi don afendin.*
Η πολλή δουλειά τρώει τον αφέντην.
Too much work can kill you.

4. *Ivres don ayion soo, na apsis do jerin soo.*
Ηβρες τον άγιον σου ν' άψεις το τζερί σου.
You found your saint to light your candle.

5. *I alooboo efaen da gadoorimena dis.*
Η αλουπού έφαεν τα κατουρημένα της.
The fox ate what she pissed on.
English: **What goes around comes around.**

6. *I alooboo ston ibnon dis ethhoren bedinarga.*
Η αλουπού στον ύπνον της εθώρεν πετεινάρκα.
The fox was dreaming of chickens.

7. *I kali mera fenede boo do broin.*
Η καλή μέρα φαίνεται που το πρωί.
The fine day shows from the morning.

8. *Iban doo belloo na shiesi, Je evkalen je da andera doo.*
Είπαν του πελλού να σιέσει τζ' έφκαλεν τζαι τ' άντερα του.
They told a fool to have a shit, and he pushed his intestines out.

9. *Iben o yaros doo bedinoo, jefala.*
Είπεν ο γάρος του πετεινού τζεφάλα.
The donkey called the rooster big-headed.

10. *I ylossa gokkala then ehi je gokkala tsakkizi.*
Η γλώσσα κόκκαλα δεν έχει τζαι κόκκαλα τσακκίζει.
The tongue has no bones, but crushes bones.

11. *I gali loargasmi **ga**mnoon doos gal**oo**s filoos.*
Οι καλοί λοαρκασμοί κάμνουν τους καλούς φίλους.
Good agreements make good friends.

12. *I niffi brin na yennithi dis bethheras dis mia**z**i.*
Η νύμφη πριν να γεννίθεί της πεθθεράς ημοιάζει.
The bride looks like her mother-in-law before she is even born.

13. *Irtan da **a**rga na vgaloon da **i**mera.*
Ηρταν τ' άρκα να φκάλουν τα ήμερα.
The feral came and chased the domestic.

14. *Inda anemos efisisen jeferesse thag**a**do.*
Ηντ' άνεμος εφύσησεν τζ' έφερε σε δακάτω.
What wind blew you our way?

15. *I aban**di**si doo bell**oo** en i si**o**bi.*
Η απάντηση του πέλλού εν η σιωπή.
Silence is the best way to deal with an idiot.

16. *I bandr**i**a en llah**i**on.*
Η παντρειά ε'λλαχείον.
Marriage is lottery.

17. *I az**oo**la an idan b**oo**za, itan na bo**o**ziasi o kosmos **oo**los.*
Η αζούλα αν ήταν πούζα ήταν να πουζιάσει ο κόσμος ούλλος.
If jealousy was a hernia, the whole world would have had a hernia.

J

Page 229 to 238

1. *Ji boo gra**z**oon bolli bedini argi na ksimerosi.*
Τζίει που κράζουσιν πολλοί πετεινοί αρκεί να ξημερώσει.
Too many roosters delay the dawn.
English version: **Too many cooks spoil the broth.**

2. *Jiame boo ise imoon, je thame boo ime ennartis.*
Τζιαμέ που είσαι ήμουν τζιαι τζιαμέ που είμα εν νάρτεις.
Where you are I have been, and where I am you will be.

3. *Jinos papas, jinos dadas.*
Τζιείνος παπάς, τζιείνος τατάς.
He is the priest and the godfather.

4. *Jiloon davgon me din manavellan.*
Τζιυλούν τ' αυκόν με την μαναβέλλαν.
They roll an egg with a beam.

5. *Jinos bon se kseri, agriva se yorazi.*
Τζείνος πον σε ξέρει, ακριβά σε γοράζει.
If one doesn't know you well, one would invest dearly on you.

K

Page 239 to 240

1. *Ksenos golos oson thelis htiba.*
Ξένος κώλος όσο θέλεις χτύπα.
Someone else's buttock, smack as much as you like.

L

Page 241 to 247

1. *Lamne broin is din thoolian je anoras is do spidin.*
Λάμνε πρωίν εις τη δουλειά τζ' ανώρας εις το σπίτι.
Work early in the morning and go home early.

2. *Lamne mavroirevke.*
Λάμνε μαυροϋρεφκε.
Go surging in the dark. English: **Mind your own business.**

3. *Lali do i gargia doo.*
Λαλεί το η καρκιά του.
He's got guts.

4. *Libi o Martis boo din saracosdin?*
Λείπει ο Μάρτης που τη Σαρακοστήν;
March is never absent from Lent.

5. *Libi o gattos je i bondiji horevgoon.*
Λείπει ο κάττος τζαι οι ποντιτζιοί χορεύκουν.
The mice are dancing while the cat slacks off.

6. *Loargazoosin horis don ksenothohon.*
Λοαρκάζουσιν χωρίς τον ξενοδόχο.
Making plans without the host.

M

Page 249 to 274

1. *Ma nomizis bos en do hanin doo Ppanjaroo?*
Μα νομίζεις εν το χάνι του Ππάντζιαρου;
Do you think this is the Panjarou's hostel?

2. *Mathhe dehnin je gremmasdin is do balloojin.*
Μάθε την τέχνη τζαι κρέμμαστην στο παλλούτσιν.
Learn a trade and hang it on the hook.

3. *Mathhe yiero yrammada.*
Μάθε γέρο γράμματα.
You can't teach an old man how to read and write.
English equivalent: **You can't teach old dog new tricks.**

4. *Mmathkia boo then vleboonde efgola ksehnioonde.*
Μάθκια που δεν βλέπουνται γλήορα ξεχνιούνται.
Eyes that cannot be seen are easily forgotten.

5. *Me din millan mas, dianizi do vlanjin mas.*
Με τη μίλλα μας τηανίζει το βλαντζί μας.
With our fat fries our liver.

6. *Me don thkiaolon na tho, me don stavron moo na gamo.*
Με τον δκιάολον να δω, με τον σταυρό μου να κάμω.
Neither the devil to see, nor the sign of the cross to do.

7. *Me don noon doo gamni bairamin.*
Με τον νουν του κάμνει παϊράμι.
Is celebrating a Ramadan in his own mind.

8. *Men biannis do psoomin boo do stoman don bethkion doo belecanoo.*
(Belecanos=carpenter, From the Greek verb *beleco* = craft or hew wood.)
Μεν πιάννεις το ψουμί που το στόμα των παιδκιών του πελεκάνου.
Do not take the bread from the mouth of the carpenter's children.

9. *Me da millosfonjismada ththeloon na gamoon bittes.*
Με τα μιλλοσφοντσίσματα θέλουν να κάμουν πίττες.
They want to make pita bread from an oily rug.

10. *Mealon vookkon vale ma mealon lon men bis.*
Μιάλον βούκκον βάλε, μιάλον λόον μεμ' πεις.
Take a big bite but don't make a big statement.

11. *Men soozis da bothkia soo brin na gavallijebsis.*
Μεν σούζεις τα πόδκια σου πριν να καβαλλιτσέψεις.
Do not dangle your legs before you ride on the horse.

12. *Men akannis do sherin boo se daizi.*
Μεν ακκάννεις το σιέριν που σε ταΐζει.
Do not bite the hand that feeds you.

13. *Me doo psilloo ppiiman.*
Με του ψύλλου ππήδημα.
With just a flea's leap.

14. *Me don zorin o shillos en bianni laon.*
Με το ζόριν ο σιύλλος εν πιάννει λαόν.
You cannot force a dog to catch a hare.
English equivalent: **You can take a horse to the water, but you can't make it drink.**

15. *Me singenin soo fae bie, ma alishi verishi men gamis.*
Με συγγενή σου φάε πιε, μα αλίσιν βερίσιν μεν κάμεις.
With relatives drink and party, but don't do business with.

16. *Medra thkio fores je gopse mian.*
Μέτρα δκυο φορές τζαι κόψε μιαν.
Measure twice and cut once.

17. *Mbros gremmos je biso remma.*
Ομπρός κρεμμός τζαι πίσω ρέμα.
We are between a cliff and a ravine.

N

Page 275 to 279

1. *Na bierosi en ebierosen je yirevgi je resta.*
Να πιερώσει εν επιέρωσεν τζαι γυρεύκει τζαι ρέστα.
He didn't even pay and is asking for change.

2. *Na vgi do yieman do bellon.*
Να βκει το γαίμαν το πελλόν.
Let the foolish blood come out.

3. *Nisdiji i argootha en horevgi.*
Νηστιτσή η αρκούδα εν χορεύκει.
A hungry bear doesn't dance.

O

Page 281 to 335

1. O bathos en o yiadros.
Ο παθός εν ο γιατρός.
The sufferer is the doctor.

2. Obos sdrosis etsi en na jimithis.
Οπως στρώσεις έτσι εν να τζοιμηθείς.
You sleep the way you do your bed.
In English: **You made your bed, you lie in it.**

3. O foornos doo Nastradin Hojia.
Ο φούρνος του Ναστραδίν Χότζια.
The wood-fired oven of Nastradin Hodjia.

4. O yaros o gondris ama thi do sdradoorin voora.
Ο γάρος ο κόντρης άμα δει το στρατούρι βουρά.
A donkey with blisters runs away at the sight of a saddle.
Similar to the English: **He has a chip on his shoulder.**

5. O aloobos ehonnedoon Je o nooros do idan bokso.
Ο αλουπός εχώννετουν τζ' ο νούρος του ήταν πόξω.
The fox was hiding and his tail was out.

6. O Thheos ayaba je don gleftin, ayaba je don nigojirin.
Ο Θεός αγαπά τζαι τον κλέφτην, αγαπά τζαι τον νοικοτζύρην.
God loves the thief but also loves the housekeeper.

7. Oson miso da gardama sta yenia moo vlasdoosin.
Οσο μισώ τα κάρταμα στα γένια μου βλαστούσιν.
The more I hate cress, the more they grow on my face.

8. Odi dreksi as gadevasi.
Οτι τρέξει ας κατεβάσει.
Whatever run will run.

9. *O galos o filos odan don hriazese fenede.*
Ο καλός ο φίλος όταν τον χρειάζεσαι φαίνεται.
A friend in need is a friend indeed.

10. *O galos o gabedanios sdin foordoonan fenede.*
Ο καλός ο καπετάνιος στη φουρτούνα φαίνεται.
Used when a talker faces an opportunity to show action.

11. *O galos o drobos vcalli je din goofin boo din driban dis.*
Ο καλός ο τρόπος φκάλλει τζαι την κουφήν που την τρύπαν της.
Kindness can make even a snake friendly.

12. *O kattos jan eyerasen da nishia boo ishen eshi.*
Ο κάττος τζ' αν εγέρασεν τα νύσια πούσιεν έσιει.
The old cat still has his old claws.

13. *O cosmos doshi doombanon je emis grifon gamarin.*
Ο κόσμος τώσιει τούμπανο τζ' εμείς κρυφό καμάριν.
Our precious secret everyone knows.

14. *O nooros doo shilloo en ishionni.*
Ο νούρος του σιύλλου εν ισιώννει.
You can't straighten up a dog's tail.

15. *O bellos boo din bordan.*
Ο πελλός που την πόρταν.
The foolish with the door.

16. *Oboo eshi gabnon eshi je fulhkian.*
Οπου έσιει καπνόν έσιει τζαι φωδκιάν.
Where there is smoke there is fire.

17 *O fovos ferni golasin.*
Ο φοος φερνει κολασην.
Fear brings hell.

18. Obi**o**s jini**a** thki**o** la**oo**s, h**a**nni d**oo**s je d**oo**s thki**o**.
Οποιος τζυνηά δκιο λαούς, χάννει τους τζαι τους δκιο.
Who hunts two rabbits at the same time, loses them both.

19. O bell**o**s ebojimithhin, je bell**o**n **o**roman ithen.
Ο πελλός εποτσοιμήθην τζαι πελλόν ορομαν είδεν.
The foolish had a foolish dream.

20. O ps**e**ftis je o gl**e**ftis don br**o**don hr**o**non sheroonde.
Ο ψεύτης τζαι ο κλέφτης τον πρώτον χρόνον σιαίρουνται.
Liars and thieves are happy only the first year.
English equivalent: **You can fool some people sometimes, but not all people all the time.**

21. Obios ann**i**i don l**a**kkon doo **a**lloo p**e**fti o **i**thios mesa.
Οποιος αννοίει τον λάκκον του άλλου, ππέφτει ο ίδιος μέσα.
Who opens someone else's grave falls in it himself.

22. Obios anacad**o**nnete me da b**i**dera dr**o**ndon i **o**rnithhes.
Οποιος ανακατώννεται με τα πίτερα τρων' τον οι όρνιθες.
If you mix with the chicken food, you get eaten by chicken.

23. Obios theli da b**o**lla h**a**nni je da ll**i**a.
Οποιος θέλει τα πολλά, χάννει τζαι τα λλία.
Who wants the lot, loses even the few.

24. O g**o**los o d**i**tsiros **i**then do vraj**i**n je esh**e**stin.
Ο κώλος ο ανεβράκωτος είδεν το βρατσίν τσ' εσιέστην.
The naked buttock saw underpants and shat itself.

25. O y**a**ros mian foran goodoolla sto thendron je boir**i**zi.
Ο γάρος μια φορά κουτουλλά στο δέντρον τζαι πουρίζει.
A donkey hits a tree once, never goes past it again.

26. O y**a**ros o ogni**a**ris, **e**n je vari yomark**a**ris.
Ο γάρος ο οκνιάρης εν τζαι βαρυγομαρκάρης.
The lazy donkey overloads himself.

27. Ola dahe i Mariori**,** o ferejes tis elibe.
Ολα τάσιει η Μαριορή, ο φερετσές της λείπει.
Marjory had everything gone wrong, and still wanted a Burka.

28. Osa ban je osartoon.
Οσα παν τζ' όσα έρτουν.
An uncontrolled situation.

29. O shillos boo lassi, en akkanni.
Ο σιύλλος που λάσσει εν ακκάννει.
Dogs that bark don't bite.

30. O shillos ji boo droi, ji lassi.
Ο σιύλλος τζει που τρώει τζει λάσσει.
The dog barks where he eats.

31. Obios viazete scondafti
Οποιος βιάζεται σκοντάφτει.
Who rushes trips.

32. Obios en thheli na zimosi bende meres goshinizi.
Οποιος εν θέλει να ζυμώσει πέντε μέρες κοσιηνίζει.
Who doesn't want to bake sifts for five days.

33. O voscos o pseftis.
Ο βοσκός ο ψεύτης.
The lying shepherd.
English equivalent: **Crying wolf.**

34. Oolli l**e**sin je bol**e**n, je o ftoh**o**s ji boo bon**i**.
Ούλλοι λέσιν τζαι πολέν τζ' ο φτωχός τζει που πονεί.
Everybody about the issue, and the poor about his pain.

35. Oolli yia din mana mas rodoon.
Ούλλοι για την μάνα μας ρωτουν.
All men are interested only for our mother.

36. *Oboo ibarhi thelisi, ibarhi je o drobos.*
Οπου υπάρχει θέλειση, υπάρχει τζαι ο τρόπος.
Where there is a will, there is a way.

P

Page 337 to 338

1. *Psahni yia psilloos mes d'ashera.*
Ψάχνει για ψύλλους μες τ' άσιερα.
Looking for nits in the haystack.
English version: **Looking for needles in the haystack.**

S

Page 339 to 349

1. *Spire na ttherisis.*
Σπύρε να θερίσεις.
Sow to harvest.

2. *Stoo coofoo din borda, oso tthelis vronda.*
Στου κουφού την πόρτα όσο θέλεις βρόντα.
On the deaf man's door knock as much as you like.

3. *Stoos difloos vasilevi o monofthhalmos.*
Στους τυφλούς βασιλεύει ο μονόφθαλμος.
In the kingdom of blind the one-eyed is a king.

4. *Stin anerkan fela je do halazin.*
Στην ανερκάν φελά τζαι το χαλάζι.
In the drought hail will do.

5. *Sirne avka bass don dihon, golloon?*
Σύρνε αυκά πας τον τοίχον, κολλούν;
Throw eggs on the wall, do they stick?

6. *Shillon blinnis shillon loosis, bale shilies mirizi.*
Σιύλλον πλύννεις, σιύλλον λούσεις, πάλαι σιυλλιές μυρίζει.
A dog would always smell like a dog even if you wash it.

T

Page 351 to 366

1. *Thheli je do psoomin soston je don shillon hortadon.*
Θέλει τζαι το ψουμί σωστό τζαι τον σιύλλο χορτάτον.
He wants the bread whole and the dog fed.
English version: You can't have your **cake and eat it too.**

2. *Theli golajion do moron, na vali noon me don jeron.*
Θέλει κολατσιόν το μωρό, να βάλει νουν με τον τζαιρόν.
Be gentle with kids; they'll mature in time.

3. *Thimos doo horkadi, zimia doo boonjioo doo.*
Θυμός του χωρκάτη, ζημιά του πουντζού του.
Villager's anger is loss to his purse.

4. *Thos doo belloo loocanicon, je na soo be ma en zavon.*
Δως του πελλού λουκάνικον τζαι να σου πει μα εν ζαβόν.
Give a fool a sausage to complain that it's not straight.

5. *Thos doo tharros doo horkadi, jenna mbi me des boines mes'do grevadin.*
Δώστου θάρρος του χωρκάτη τζ' εννά μπει με τες ποϊνες στο κρεβάτι.
Encourage the villager, and he is in bed boots and all.
English equivalent: **Give him your finger, and he will grab your hand.**

6. *Thakkanni donan, je bonoon don oolla.*
Δακκάννει τόναν τζαι πονούν τον ούλα.
He bites the one (finger), and they all heard.

7. *Thame se thelo gavoora, na drappias da garvoona.*
Δαμέ σε θέλω κάβουρα να τραππιάς τα κάρβουνα.
Here you are, crab, jump out of the fire.

8. *Thaskale boo thithaskes, je nomon then egrades.*
Δάσκαλε που δίδασκες τζαι νόμον εν εκράτες.
Teacher, practise what you preach.

9. *Thigon moo yaoorin, obos thelo thinno do.*
Δικό μου γαούριν, όπου θέλω δίννω το.
My donkey, I tie it the way I like.

10. *Thos moo jira don andran soo, je soo ame na vris allon.*
Δώσ'μου τζυρά τον αντρα σου τζαι σου αμε νάβρεις άλλον.
Lady, give me your husband, and you go seek another.

V

Page 367 to 377

1. *Vaose je romanise, je obothhen thhelis emba.*
Βάωσε τζαι ρομάνισε τζ' όποθθεν θέλεις έμπα.
Lock up the house and walk in from anywhere.

2. *Valli boo d'onan je vkalli boo do allon.*
Βάλλει που τόναν τζαι φκάλλει που τάλλον.
In from one ear and out the other.

3. *Vkenni bobano san do lain.*
Φκέννει πουπάνω σαν το λάϊν.
Rises on top, like oil.

4. *Vlebis thkio je en mallonnoon, eksere bos en boo don enan.*
Βλέπεις δκιο τζ' εν μαλλώνουν, έξερε πως εν που τον έναν.
If a couple don't quarrel, it is because of the one.

5. *Voora, je en siftanni.*
Βουρά τζ' εν συφταίννει.
Bursting and running.

6. *Voonon me voonon en ismii.*
Βουνόν με βουνόν εν ησμίει.
Two mountains do not meet.

7. *Vlebe erga k'ohi loyia.*
Βλέπε έργα τζ' όϊ λόγια.
See action not talk.
English version: **All talk but no action.**

8. *Voora na deliosis je ade na da mballosis.*
Βούρα να τελιώσεις τζαι άτε να μπαλλώσεις.
Rush to finish and sit to repair.

Y

Page 379 to 389

1. *Yidon eshis, Thheon eshis.*
Γείτον έσιεις, Θεόν έσιεις.
You have a good neighbour, you have God.

2. *Yia do hattirin dis vasilijias, binni i ylastra do neron.*
Για το χαττίριν της βασιλιτσιάς πίννει η γλάστρα το νερό.
For basil's sake, you water the pot.

3. *Yiati en thigon doo gavki don, yiati do rizi kshi don.*
Γιατί εν δικόν του καύκει τον, γιατί το ρίζει ξιεί τον.
Because it's his, it burns him, and because he owns it, he cares.

4. *Yia migros migros bandreftoo, yia migros galoireftoo.*
Για μικρός-μικρός παντρεύτου για μικρός καλοηρεύτου.
Get married young, or become a monk young.

5. *Yia don psillon gavgoon do babloman.*
Για τον ψύλλον καύκουν το πάπλωμα.
For a nit they burn the doona.

6. *Yia na se bethhimoosin, arke llion na se thoosin.*
Για να σε πεθυμούσιν, άρκε λλίο να σε δούσιν.
If you want them to miss you, see them rarely

7. *Yleboo na se ylebi je o Thheos.*
Γλέπου να σε γλέπει τζ' ο Θεός.
God will protect you if you take care of yourself.

8. *Yiorti moo emenan, baramoni thiki soo.*
Γιορτή μου εμένα, παραμονή δική σου.
My celebration, the eve of yours.

9. *Yirevki psilloos mes d'ashera.*
Γυρεύκει ψύλλους μες τ' άσιερα.
Looking for nits in the haystack.
English version: **Looking for needles in the haystack.**

PHONETICS ORTHOGRAPHY CHART

In order to achieve maximum phonetical accuracy in pronouncing the Greek Cypriot expressions, English characters must be pronounced as per chart below.

graphems					phonems	Greek
a	pronounced as in				**a**pple	α
e	"	"	"	"	**e**lephant	ε
g	"	"	"	"	**g**ood	κ
i	"	"	"	"	**i**nk	ι
y	"	"	"	"	**y**ellow	γ
oo	"	"	"	"	z**oo**	ου
th	"	"	"	"	**th**e	δ
thh	"	"	"	"	**th**ick	θ
b	"	"	"	"	**b**aby	π
p	"	"	"	"	**P**eter	ππ

Acc**e**ntuate on b**o**lder v**o**wels.

Example: (for English speaking readers only)

Esi B**e**tro then br**e**bi na g**a**nis thh**o**rivo me do booz**oo**ki soo ab**o**bse yia na min ksibn**i**sis da migr**a** mor**a**gia boo gim**oo**nde.

Printed in Australia
AUOC02n1625070416
275041AU00001B/1/P